CW01572952

1.50

Ngl

A Poetic Journey
copyright © Keith Harris 2022
ISBN 978-1-903466-21-6

This book is published by *Pending Press* Ltd.

A Poetic Journey

Keith Harris

Published by **Pending Press** Ltd.

Dedication

This book is dedicated to
the Maid of the Mystic Now

Contents

May a star shine on our meeting

Preface

Is it possible to write a complete poem in just three lines? Definitely, just consider Basho's:

An ancient pool's silence
broken as a frog springs into water
gentle resonance

Is it possible to write a whole book of linked poems carried by a forward motion and drawing to a kind of conclusion ... and yet for the work to feel truncated, unfinished or unprepared?

This problem I have striven to overcome since the late Nineteen Eighties because the books of linked poetry: *Armoured to Anonymity, Cupid's Anon, Colours in Chiaroscuro, Hegelian Fragments, Tomorrow Troubling Today, Arthur I and II, Guinevere and The Lady's Maid* were never complete in themselves. For me they comprise a single whole. Sadly with a family of young children and full-time work I was unable to put these poems together into one book. Lamely I produced each of the above books separately. Now that each in itself is finished, I can do the book I always envisaged namely this one: *A Poetic Journey.*

For me the above sequences of linked verse are themselves only really viable when set together into a greater whole.

We are living in the Third Millennium and literature cannot really be divorced from the time in which it came into being. *Armoured to Anonymity* is dislocated from the Twentieth and Twenty-first Centuries because it was meant to flow into *Cupid's Anon* and *Colours in Chiaroscuro* and this is again meant to wander into the lifeless byways of the Geneticist and the ribald absurdity of *Hegelian*

Fragments which is meant to grind toward the alienation encountered in *Tomorrow Troubling Today*. Yet all these sequences of linked poetry were there primarily to prepare for the poems in *Arthur, Guinevere* and *The Lady's Maid*. It is hard to conceive how someone off the street could pick up the Arthurian verses and come to terms with them. For me their meaning lies in completing the path traversed in the aforementioned books. Without this sense of journeying toward something I can only assume that readers would shake their heads or shrug their shoulders when confronting the Celtic imagery with its overtones of what lies behind sense-perceptual surfaces.

For nigh thirty five years I lived with the notion that the poems constituted a whole. Yet when I finally read through the sections from start to finish I was forced to accept that a gulf still resided between the Arthurian verses and those preceeding it.

So many of the poems in the earlier sections bear an impersonal quality. The exceptions being in *Hegelian Fragments* but here the narrating personality is that of someone dreaming. I came to feel therefore that an intermediate section of more consciously personal poetry was essential to bridge the chasm to the Arthurian conclusion. And yet I had zero inspiration as to what this might be. Until the idea came to me that it might be possible to stitch together some of my own earlier poetry. Thus *Maybe Lost* came about. Some of the poems here are newly composed (2022) others were written years ago.

Thus the sequence now stands as: *Armoured to Anonymity, Cupid's Anon, Colours in Chiaroscuro, Hegelian Fragments, Tomorrow Troubling Today, Maybe Lost, Arthur I* and *II, Guinevere* and *The Lady's Maid*.

It is quite possible to pick up a novel and dip into it, to read a chapter there, a paragraph there. But if you do this you lose the momentum of moving through the narrative. Of course readers of this book are free to browse, to read a poem here or there. But if they do this then the quality of journeying will be lost. And for me this book is first and foremost a poetic journey.

Introduction
to the Sequences of Linked Poetry

It is with a reluctance that I write short introductions to each of the sequences of linked poems. Yet I feel obliged to set the scene for each work. And I do it here in order not to hold the reader back from the path through the poetry once the journey has begun.

I have very slightly trimmed, pruned and also planted just a few new lines in the poems but otherwise they are hardly changed from their first publications.

Armoured to Anonymity

Armoured to Anonymity is a sequence of linked poems. The setting, nominally at least, is Arthur's Celtic Britain.

The poems deal with a rider's attempts to combat darkness in the outer world and in himself by following the lonely 'Arthurian' quest.

They also deal with the relationship between 'day' and 'night'.

Cupid's Anon

These poems seek to live the very moment of falling in love, hence the title: Cupid's Anon.

Colours in Chiaroscuro

A central theme is taken from Goethe's theory that colour comes into being though the dramatic interplay of light and dark – or by analogy between black and white. All the poems here have titles.

Hegelian Fragments

An introduction is necessary here if only to point out that the *Hegel* who appears in these pages is a fantasy figure definitely not to be equated with the great philosopher of German Idealism.

The poem is written as a dream sequence so the narrative is freed from many of the constraints which tether the objective world. The poem's *Hegel* is conjured up by the imagination or dreaming of the first person narrator (who should not simply be equated with me, the author, either!).

You might ask: Why set a fantasy figure in the place of an historical person?

A deeply felt question lives behind this poem which is connected with what, I am convinced, was a partial miscarriage of Hegelian philosophy.

Hegelian logic deals with the dynamic interplay between thesis and antithesis which allows a higher synthesis to present itself. The Austrian philosopher and educationalist, Rudolf Steiner, went as far as to describe Hegelian logic as an 'Eternal Logic'. The question which springs to mind is this: How was it possible for Hegel to have brought forth such a vibrant and living logic, only to rest the edifice of his philosophical and historical speculation upon 'the Absolute' – a construction akin to Monophysitism in theology.

His logic deals with the balancing of polarity but his philosophical-historical system bases itself upon a single absolute pole!

Is it possible to conceive of a greater abyss separating Hegel the philosopher of logic from Hegel meditating upon the ultimate foundations of history?

So long as we are dealing with rarefied nineteenth

century Idealist philosophy we can look at this incongruity with amused wonder. But, and this is a very big but, Hegel's philosophy not only made its presence felt in academic circles it profoundly affected the history of the twentieth century, it affected the lives of billions of people.

Karl Marx embraced Hegelian logic but turned the whole edifice of the philosophy upside down; for Marx the impetus of history is not an 'archetypal first cause' but Materialism, the grind of economics – work, production, consumption.

My suggestion is that it was possible for Marx to do this only because his teacher, Hegel, had already turned away from his first love, from the dialectical balancing of polarities, to envisage an absolute spiritual pole active behind the scenes of history. Marx in essence only brought forth the counter-pole to Hegel's ghostly Absolute.

Yet in doing this Marx also forgot the need for balance. Thus he was able to come up with the concept of the 'Dictatorship of the Proletariat' without realising this needed to be balanced. Today we are well aware of the need for the legislative, executive and judicial domains of the State to possess a high degree of independence. Marxist socialism in the twentieth century saw the Party (or the Central Committee of the Party or even the General Secretary or Chairman of the Party) as being able to speak for the people as a whole. Power became concentrated in a single point, a single person … all because Marx, like his mentor Hegel, forgot the principle of the balancing of polarities and allowed an absolute pole to dominate his thinking.

Chinese wisdom is based on the balancing of the Yang-Yin polarity. Life continues healthily if this balance is maintained. Yet Hegel's logic heralded something genuinely new: the higher synthesis, the birth of what was not previously present. This is an inherently Christian logic based upon the triune principle of birth not upon a Monophysite-like Absolutism or an ever-continuing, never-ending realignment of two formative principles.

A tragedy crosses the course of nineteenth century German Idealism. Was not this movement, with names such as Schelling, Schopenhauer, Fichte, the philosopher-scientist Henrik Steffans, the poet, philosopher and scientist Novalis, and Hegel himself, 'meant' to have grasped Goethe's method of undertaking scientific investigation, linked this to mathematics and brought forth a natural science capable of coming to grips not only with matter but the life forces imbuing nature which transform her into more than an array of particles?

German Idealist philosophy did not come to full maturity, the principle of triune balancing was orphaned.

We see Hegel turning away from the triune to embrace an abstract absolute pole. We see this subtly leading Marx toward envisaging economic activity as the single driving force behind historical progress – and we see modern science utterly in the grip of materialism.

Genetics has evolved from an analogous one-sidedness to that which finally consumed Hegel, which took over Marx and which holds modern science entranced. The figure of the Geneticist can be seen as personifying the technology deriving from a science hypnotised by materialism.

This poem in no way seeks to come to grips with the question as to why the historical individual, Hegel, renounced the dialectical balancing of polarity when he thought up his ghostly 'Absolute'. I leave that to biographers, historians and philosophers. My intention is only to create a kind of caricature, a figure all-too-human and indeed almost farcical. And if this seems harsh on the great philosopher, let his followers explain – perhaps to the hundreds of millions of human beings who suffered under 'the Dictatorship of the Proletariat' – why Hegel ultimately chose to turn away from the triune in order to embrace a single absolute pole.

The failings and frailties of the character 'Hegel' in this poem could perhaps be conceived as a kind of personification of corresponding weaknesses in the Idealist philosopher's theory of history rather than having anything to do with his biography as such.

If you assume, from reading this preface, that this is some kind of philosophical poem, let me say it deals much more with the absurd and only occasionally touches the realm of philosophy.

The poem opens with the figure of the Geneticist and moves in roundabout ways to Hegel, Marx, Stalin, Merlin only to return briefly to Hegel and the Geneticist before the narrator finally awakens.

Readers are left to judge for themselves as to whether or not a wellspring of philosophical yearning lives behind the lines of the poem.

I hope readers neither forget the name of the philosopher, Hegel, nor the magic of his momentous achievement: the triune balancing of polarities. Some might even feel the inclination to browse through his *Science of Logic*.

The figure of Merlin appears in these poems and a reference is made to the following: **The Legend of Merlin Bewitched into the Oak Tree** which tells of how Merlin *fell into a dotage of love for a certain damsel of the Lady of the Lake*. She learnt his magic crafts then one day when they were sitting together under an oak tree in the forest of Broeliande, despite his initial

reluctance she drew forth from him some of his most potent spells – *in the end her prayers and kisses overcame him, and he told her all. Then did she make him great cheer, but anon, as he lay down to sleep, she softly rose, and walked about him waving her hands and muttering the charm*, the charm which would lock the living man into the oak tree he was sleeping beside. *And therefrom nevermore could he by any means come out for all the crafts that he could do. And so she departed and left Merlin.*
(The quotations in italics are from Sir James Knowles' retelling of the Arthurian legends.)

Tomorrow Troubling Today

The poems begin with an acute sense of being cut off. This kind of feeling is perhaps even more prevalent today than when I began to write the poems in the late nineteen eighties. They represent the low-point in the whole sequence of the books of poetry mentioned above. It only remains to add that the gloom does lighten a little toward the end.

Maybe Lost

No words of introduction are written here for these poems.

Arthur, Guinevere and the Lady's Maid

An introduction is definitely needed here because otherwise the themes are likely to be misunderstood. This is not romantic, epic or lyrical poetry. The verse can only be classified as poetry of the Night not of the Day.

Are the figures of Arthur and Guinevere allegorical? Is Arthur the male and Guinevere the female side of our own human natures? Perhaps. But I hope they may be conceived symbolically with more than one interpretation.

9

Could Arthur be the physical and Guinevere the ethereal? Could Arthur be the intellect and Guinevere the soul? We can say that Arthur is king and Guinevere queen of the realm of Albion ... but this only begs the question of how 'Albion' is to be interpreted?

We can definitely say that the poems are Arthurian in the sense that Celtic Britain and the stories of the Round Table and the Grail quest set the scene. I have decided not to put in references. Those familiar with the Arthurian and Grail legends, with the Bible, William Blake and the Christian esoteric tradition springing especially from Rudolf Steiner and Valentin Tomberg can easily detect wider contexts.

Though I will mention here Arthur's sword, Excalibur. To calibrate is to measure, to be "ex-calibratable" is thus to be immeasurable and so Excalibur can be considered limitless. Arthur draws a sword from stone and in doing this he is recognised as the true king. This sword breaks. It is replaced by the sword from the Lake. The swords of stone and water. The swords of the knights defend the realm from evil and aggression just as the white blood cells defend the body from external encroachment and disease. While the red cells offer maternal sustenance to the rest of the organism. Symbolically speaking we might argue that 'the white wine' defends and 'the red wine' sustains the well being of the organism.

Near the borders of day and night the forces of the blood flow into human sexuality. The Freudian analyst is intent on uncovering the phallic element. But did not Jung, a psychoanalyst with a hungering for the mystical, say that the phallus itself is a symbol? An image perhaps also for forces active within the immune system's (k)nightly defenders of the human organism. Yet the blood can only care for our organism when the white and the red forces are in balance, that is, when male and female processes in our organism work harmoniously together.

At the opening of the Third Millennium we are beginning to realise that we can only truly be human if the male and female sides of our nature are in balance. Just as we recognise that the forces of the child within us are needed if our adult selves are not to ossify. We might even express it thus, the forces of the night need to fructify those of the day.

This harmony between the male and the female on the one hand and between childhood and ageing on the other does not come about of itself. Are not great though hidden deeds even now being done at the boundaries where the Day and the Night encounter each other? And is it not possible that these encounters could become the stuff of poetry?

Throughout these poems there is a play on the words 'night' and 'knight'. Sometimes I have not even been sure myself which spelling to use.

Armoured to Anonymity

1

Armoured to anonymity a lonely
rider whose path his
destiny decides.

2

Through wilderness and towns, through crowds
and restrictions and divisions
of families, races, nations, guilds
… and on
to pass unnoticed behind a
solitary homestead in the hills
as the West's rosy shimmering
slips toward the sea
and dark quietens
unsteady colour.

3

Iron-clad and mounted
on the grey and foamy mare
leading a trusted sandy steed
loosely laden with his needs
upon a gently-inclined weaving
ancient way
not overgrown though little used
and bordered by new green
from where white flowers face
the cloudless blue and fragrant
shrubs offer the wayfarer
refreshing sense.

His gaze wavering in distances
back to the tradesmen's bustle
and the towns then on
toward lonely Celtic moors
where mountains and seaborne mists
mean movement in the lonelier life.

4

From afar he trails a diligent trail
from whence day is freed
in rosy dawn to whither
eve's magenta bows
toward the midnight sun.
And his ascending once more
… descends
to mourn with each new morn.

By sunlight riding further
alone and on,
threading with his self
through day's display
to settle and abide
in dusk-awakened scents beside
the moonlight's wavy musing
and the silent music
of a Celtic mere.

5

Memories break as waves
throughout his trials to step
determined steps to where –
to where his knowledge never tells.
But behind his visor
chancing change
behind his breastplate
changing chance.

6

He reins in his charging steed
to graze on greens near homes
of men half-cleansed from grime
as nature's rearing day
dwindles to stillness.
Quietly, quietly
near dwellings in sleep's
familiar ways
where women loosening the grind
labour with the lasting child.

7

His countenance a visor as he rides
to divest his days of that stealth
which lurked around his crib
and clung to his tear-strewn way
into childhood sleep.
And which still masks
riddles stamped upon his livery
unless the shadow
in himself is faced.

8

Unknown he rides
through those years
when youth stalked
by an umbra of ugliness
slowly becomes
no longer young.

9

Riding lightly to joust
through unplanned day on an
unarmed steed's easily
harnessed way.

10

He gallops his pounding
stallion with pounding
heart to the clash
of lance on steel

… in defeat:
a pauper's clod of earth
and perhaps a poor maid's sigh,

in victory:
a slight dig of spur
flanks out his further flight
toward his further frays …

11

On a main bridleway through Caledonian forest
sharp sunlight's motifs mottled and moved
by birch-leaf in the breeze as well-attended
damsels, beggar monks and traders whipping
heavy-laden mules pass by the
steel upon the horse.

In unsteady shades fantasy plays
upon the passing moment
and into troubled sleep
as they each dream
of what lives behind
the visor and the shield.

12

Dappling chances dulled in sense
how many days, disjointedly,
dreamed by
while wonder glanced
his heart against half-meetings
brooding with presences
of people unknown
and half unknown.

13

As mud splashes
from his trotting mount upon
the clogs of surely thickset men
who tightly grasp their bags.

14

As his horse's hooves
clip-clop the cobble stone
a lithe and barefoot maid with
longing look seeks
the I within the helm

15

Saddle proud rides and the norm
of easy victory let
moments march away
into sans-subject and never stalling
sequential time
but cannot cause nor erase
his seeing in sight
nor shut that sheltered door
from where a knocking echoes
with the stars of night.

16

Rumours of falsity and privilege
spit from ignorant mouths
of those who shun the need
to learn from life.
But when crude foes tailored
to joust and plunder
daughter's wares –
or when things crawl
from heathen heaths and fears
creep through hamlets cringing
near the lakeside's swirling haze –
or as anarchy plunges
all to war against all
… then led by
his steed's prophetic step
Arthur's knight from night
appears upon the ridgeway:
a silhouette
who silently heralds
the rising sun.

17

Is he young
or stern and scarred of cheek
none knows, his visor
blocks his visage.
He rides to battle in our Table's name,
only upon his seat in Camelot
does his own ever newly inscribed
name
gleam
with the glede of gold.

18

Behind his visor chancing change
behind his breastplate
changing chance –
where destiny decides with easy rein
his deed's anonymous amour
there plays to undecide.

19

Each rider, fresh as arterial redness
flowing through craving limbs,
swoons into slumber
as knightly dusk rolls nightly over day.

Is there a smile upon his sleepy face
or grim fatigue? None knows
for darkness drowses overall.
His efforts have fought his day
his night needs grace-filled sleep.

20

Polarity twines his moments
in freedhood's fighting fold:
Tight recall of knightly oath
in iron rounds of iron rush
as sword and lance clash
with the well-worn shield
And paths where hope faints
into silences before
his wanderings approach
the Castle (of the Rose
in twilight's womb)
whose night's suffer none to pass
except that he be called.

21

Who gives eve's replenishing board?
Who knows, who sees?
But the beating heart of Arthur's realm
dwells kindly over Camelot's king:
a royal priestliness chastely calm
knights the focus of our quests.

22

Oh, knightly self in heartbreak's
broken night,
of iron-plated breast and metal glove
and a visor which holds
the shadow from my face:
I to the day am knight,
to the night I am
a maiden singing
unheard songs.
Forlorn and bereft upon a turret height
I cannot lift my visor
nor cast away this spear towering
in my stony self.
Only a maid to day can knight
my maiden night
and with compassion's tear,
by kindliness neither bought nor begged,
call to this self spellbound
upon a tower of spells
and with her word,
breathing to embrace,
release this lost I's flow –
for my stony pinnacle of sleep
is severed from my day.

23

Oh, nightly self in heartbreak's
broken knight –
don't fall, don't waste your spear's quest,
wait quietly my love
my tears dissolve stone
and metal bars,
reach out gaunt knight to me
I am a maid of day to maiden knight,
don't pine bereft and forlorn
upon that tower of cold,
don't douse yourself in doom
nor quail forgetful of our quest.
Quickly the pathway is unblocked
the stairs wind slowly down,
don't wait the way is winding
but is straight and true,
beside me stands the unlocked door
its guards sob with my sorrows.
Fly my knight to me
and I will marry you to
day, come my night
the gate is open and the quest
is found or will be found
when you and I
say: *We*.

24

What did she whisper
flying from my sight as dawn's
misty Celtic twilight dissolved
and colours hardened into things,
what did she say parting from me
this cold morning grey:
When you and I learn
that togetherness lives
today.

In Autumn breezes sways
a rosebud
with a blood-red crown

Cupid's Anon

1

In breezes from far-off climes
dreams loosen one after one
unrecoverable
as falling leaves

2

From childhood memories
into this moment
a butterfly flutters
to the blue flower.

3

By a glade behind whispers
alone and longing for a chalice
the greenery hides,
my finger bruises a slender stem
and my heart is smote
with another's hurt.

4

Dreaming till my eye
slips outward
seeing to be seen.
A face first shyly
encountered
in a touch of eyes,
a face first loved
within that moment's
echo
in the now.

5

A quiver from nowhere
an absence rhyming
with a presence –
a flight of muted recognition
with dart
of the I of an eye
in me.

6

The feathery focus
of not here
magnifies
here.

7

A sensitive chaos:
Tremors
from a soundless bow
string reverberations
through a system's faltering
periodicity …
in blithe and tender
tempest
a child touches
the womb.

8

Drab turnings
round ambition's
merciless barren turn
as with ceaseless iterations
the Herod-in-me
mutilates
this moment newly
birthed.

9

Palaces of the wealthy are closed
to what is not
as it was.

In an unnoticed stall
the babe is born this night.
In caves woven with webs
of human history the
infant smiles.
And into these stony
double-spiralled stairways
sunlight shines
interceding for the in-between,
crowning with presence
what is yet to be.

10

Yet what of those other babes,
those once fresh daytimes
in displaced days
wilted with the bitter myrrh
of innocence passed on.

Tides unbecoming as incense
senses convolvuous in sense …
as the golden glow
of an eve gone by
is shrouded with
interlude.

11

Yesterday's surface tinsel
pitched
with my turning sight
into memory's vat
of vagueness.

12

As drudgery habituates
and shrinks
the coming dream
as the vague displaces
vagaries …

13

Then to then again
passed
before the future came
… to linger
as the happiness of time.

14

Until drawing through another
of many todays
Cupid's arrow flies.

15

Anonymous wings
bow minstrel music
from will be to was
through the love-riven heart
of the unfolding
in-between.

16

Whispers from the winds
winged faces hover
as our first smile
blushes
with remembrance.

17

A first sigh pregnant
with the unforgettable promise
of one alive today
who also lives
inside forgotten memories
from long, long ago.

18

Our meeting focused
by two moments in timeless
separation.

Sorrows in joy
two tears vault
arching through vanished time
toward the
happiness of now

19

The mystic troubadour:
Through my swooning self
the beloved sighs
– this song in me is yours –
and yet I cradle still
within my tenderest time
the unknown you
I love.

* * *

From a white rose petal
a tear rolls
to coalesce with dew
upon the red rosebud

* * *

Colours in Chiaroscuro

Avalon

When songs to imaginations are made
then here in Avalon a way is laid
dreaming through starry sometime climes
where maid and man without their shoes
seek sacrament in sweet débuts:
there behind those sleepy bedtime chimes
when now to a happily-ever-after cue
our prince and princess sigh to woo.

Topology

The mathematician cries:
When I was waking up this morn
as night from day was being torn
my thoughts curving such topsy-turvy waves
as stars descending into caves
but then as though abandoned in my stall
a light within me wondered if the Fall
was but God's way
to give topology its say.

The Haekkelite replies:
I know exactly what you mean
from recapitulations in the human bean
when what's first made
is tenderly out-splayed
kneaded inside so nice and thin
so what's outside is turned within.

Knightly

Where is the narrow virgin way
between staunch kingly I
and queenly dress of you,
between this mantled
queenly quiet self
and you's brave kingly build?

Is the virgin way through night
the straight and narrow vertical
which without trespassing
crosses
these horizontal lies.

The Blade in Stone

Burghers in a forgotten town
flexing huge grimaces of girth
lumber in file, gruntled with mirth,
to flourish flabby fingers flush
around the crystal hilt clutched
by grey and gravid stone.

A sword lures their tortuous bustle
with contagious greed to grip its power
a granite sheath, lust boils
to sticky pus:
Just one gruff lurch of will
and I'll rip from rock's foster
the blade in stone
and weigh all ways as mine
smelling this hour my ego
fills out all space and history,
this, this unbounded
boundless me.

Each bows to rob
only to retreat,
blank life blinks
shuttering inflation
in a momentary niche.

Each sore with his sore
as palms lacerated by a diamond hilt
drip earthwards a healing red,
as speculations tingle
in a bruised self,
as eyes shuffle to the ground
from a centre tautened in pain.

Only a youth, unknown
to the organising baton
of an object-battened day,
bears in his pulse
a breathing name
burning its rune
on the blade in stone.

Eddies

Of ways meandering
within mazes of appetite:
Where turns of eyes
and sweets upon the lips
or dainty sighs
and party wines in sips,
where pleasured snaps
spice up our girdling plays
– or as dripping taps
rap out the passing of todays.

Collisions

Frustrations giggling
tipsily round wine-soaked twirls
as two selves colliding
tie their not-there stares
… and plummet
shorn of cadence
into rut.
Folded in flues of sweat
still the other unknown
as before.

Anticlimax

In this retiring climax of operations
tempestuous with riteless stunts
bearing on our tiring brunts
all muffled up in ruthless grunts
where man dies in his coming
and woman hardly deigns to come.

Caprice

As random tune tandems
my inattentiveness with trivia,
as wine-bar wine whisks up
plays of perkiness
and memories are cocktailed
with presentiment …

Seduction

Along this once-winsome
twisting road with Georgian
town-houses where I paraded
youth's unsought ideals
in free-fading Sixties' flowers
and urges mowed
erstwhile tomorrows
into yesterdays.

Whistling tunes
that decorated days
which saw my adolescence
wave airily to childhood
fleeing far away.

Still wandering
this same winding way
where percy played and played
while wonder wound
away from wonderland
and urges tied
what were tomorrows
into a hazy maze
of yesterdays.

The Highgate door opens
to a yesterday yuppie's
people-filled and over-partied den,
"A friend of Simon's,
well, come on in!"

Dim electric lurid glare,
smoky passages, alcoves
where decorations and decorated
female searchlights coax
libido up from loveless surfaces.

My awareness touched
by a passing tactile arm,
mask-scarred eyes brush
through the party's pumped-up cool,
her smirking yet mildly
pain-charred glance
sticks in mine.
Capriciously the champagne glass
rolls on her moist-tongue smile,
she looks away (to let me know).

As though once more
in yesterday's time I
come on …
practised exchanges
manoeuvring
our verbal intercourse.

Even here among
the yesterday yuppie's hangers-on
a third person can become
a second.
A she becomes a you.

Electrifying strobo-haze
and throbbing bobbing bass
roughs up vestibules of cool,
rapid repeating jingles beat up
the Sixties' rhythm into warmed-up
ecstatic techno-thrills,
dancing's no longer just a way
to say hello as on the floor
close up affectations
of pelvic sensitivity
are affected
by the bonking beat.

Hard gets high on soft
and time is pressed … till
in some dark smoky corner or on
a sports car's springy back-seat sponge we
begin to chug.

Tongues slurp in open lips
as wildly exercising
drifts of our hands over us
we approach the verge
where depths unexorcised
gape
around erection …
as I unsteady in myself
lean on unsteadiness in you.

Did the Sixties' too soon aged youth
first conceive philosophy in the
lonely loveless aftermath
of a shag?

Late Sixties' rampaging fun hanging
over a millennium's ending
and new beginning ...
Tell me, in the last century's
last third what was not
already flowering
(and deflowered) in the Sixties?
Am I living in a new millennium?

Did it happen, did we
meet and chug last night
or was it some spent-youth
recollection,
or did I just dream about a girl
I never had the courage to address,
an imagined encounter, an emblem
of studied masturbation
or was it allegory:
the Sixties' flower of youth
seduced, shagged out
and pensioned off, idealism
smouldering
to ashes ...

Or was it presentiment
of wastage yet to come
in this world shackled
by Thermodynamics' sterile
Second Law of warmth's
(and human warmth's)
final entropy?

Who now from the Sixties
would dare a journey through the dark
to find that spring where
wells the Silver Stream
and follow its course toward
the Lady in the Golden Wood?

Captivity

Mirrorings of digital
imprisonment
where we, you and I,
daub ourselves
in electric sight-sound
fluctuations,
soft-screech images on the
screen or virtual 3D
metaverses endlessly
fractalising …

Days cloned
on wake-up pills,
vitamin-bomb pills,
'happy pills', zap-game 'pills'
damp-down pills
with viagara-esque virtuosity
rapping on P-pill-stifled wombs
before sleeping pills
bring slumber's zombie snores …

While the global web is wove
and from the dollar's pyramid
the sleepless Eye
of Baradûr stares …

Entropy

Is this but echo
forgotten ere forgot,
blank pictures where an eye
casts no I,
where a self
habituated to the habitat
of surfaces reflectable
in a looking glass,
where an I shorn of
you asleep in me
(me sleeping in you)
is signed and numbered
as a normal personality.
That consciousness lashing its stick
of sex and anodyne anonymity
through a world glowering
with ego.

Heavy with hung-over sense
gravity downs hours
and meaning discontinues
in amalgams of separation
as vocal sounds called mine
murmur over
my ever extending
incognito,
as an I
caked in me
(cracking to be free)

cloys
exteriors of second persons,
as my hereditary conditioning
(the Herod-in-me)
lurks at the brink of sleep
and with automated response
takes pain and daytime-killing pills
to slay that still small voice
which suffers and travails
for the child lost in my limbs.

Mechanic pound
of heartless brazen pace,
have I drummed out
childhood's accordance
in heavy phrase-deleted beat
and with heavy even tramping
stamped out thankless
iterations
of this selfsame ego …
from a day of coolness
to a night of cold.

Mechanic sounds spinning
repetitions inside repetitions,
mechanic mounds of ongoing
endless monotony …

Have I rolled out my years
as sequential snakes?
Where aged by worn out drives
meaning commutes toward
probability
and laws of chance demand
grey entropy
or that slow decline
toward
the closet of
"sans everything".

Treadmills

In endless electric-lit hours where
memory mimes masquerades …
have I mangled
this moment into
tormented turns of
yesterday?

Treadmills devoid
of those respite-touches
tapering
from unborn night
to flame in time.

The While

Have I wiled away
the mystic while?

The mystic present:
where in our each heart's
encounter
my life touches you
as your life
touches mine.

Rainbows

In me your picture's secret paints
as unseen form
never still yet ever
still beyond my sight.
My vision opening to light
chances or is chanced
to meet with prayer when preying
slips away.
My eye looks from somewhere
out to somewhere,
these looks of mine which meeting
another's glance tremble
to return.
My heartbeat patiently impatient
when sad in joy
or troubled through delight.

Within my painter's sight
rainbows
come to earth and linger
as promises from paradise.
The spectrum's seven
christen
the separated nearness
of black and white.

The brush-stroke listlessly laments
as black descends on white.
Am I Othello
who painted pictures of human war
for pity welling in her inner sight,
when she seeing wounds
imagined me
and I seeing tears
saw her I?

Black on white:
White – virgin or barren?
Not yet virgin and surely
the barrenness is mine alone
in this life where charcoal
memories engrave
chiaroscuro moods.

Are you out there
or in me?
Or am I moving
married to both?
To cries of inwardness that yearn
to live though sick
with passion's dregs
and smothered
by cool-warmth
or am I wed to outward wonders
woven as a world
where I, seemingly, am
yet am not.

Once I sketched these lines
as whispers from that voice
tacitly pining
as my colours drizzle
through chiaroscuro:
Borne in my I
before my birth
your picture looks
through countless outer forms
… until
meeting with a future now
the unseen beloved sees
to see in me
– the eyes in me are yours –
and Maya's dark arthritic
claws are lost
in fires uncindering …
two flames flame
as one
and separate,
I to I …
Beatific moments
passing slowly
into time.

Beatific togetherness
transcending
the monotone transience
of time.

Yet my present-now is lame
and lives by this faith alone:
that the future to the past is hope
but the future of the present
charity.

Aged I plod the earth and paint
with eye and inner eye
but today as thence your face
dances in my shades
still fresh as roses
glowing luminously red
on Winter's bare
and blackened bark.

* * *

The Blue Flower

Through many guises, many lives
I have sought
the blue, blue flower
yet never knew
she had taken root
in the soft-scented earth
around my home
to watch so faithfully
my star.

* * *

Hegelian Fragments:
a dream sequence

1

... and prophecies he said he culled
from Merlin soaking still in Merlin's Oak
to show how soon that bridge
by which romance is borne
beyond Hegelian strife
will be annulled
and neutered in the gene:
With blocks mounted and dovetailed into blocks
patch-worked existences will heave with life
and run the rub to barren
hub-hub sounds;
baronial powerhouses of production
concealing incisions of the
nanoscopic knife
will recompose and belch
organismic smog
to fall as soot from smoke
and raining down, rein in
and strangle symbiosis;
orcismatic hordes
predators among competitors
inbred to breed so rife
and programmed
to contaminate every garden
every weed and worm
... and then to reign
and clamber over serfs.

From towers of brick laid brick on brick
which baronial contrivance well knows
can be live-stocked with
transhumanistic creatures, bio-machine
men nursed on mechanistic tits.
Under ubiquitous surveillance
the post-industrial (genetic)
revolution will be initiated.

He took a doll whose hair was grass
and flowers eyes, and as he spoke
he slowly pulverised her breast
she faintly choked with vivisected cries
and trembled in his hands so plaintively.
His fingers were thin and seemed to grope
and as they dug, his nails
were lacquered and were long.

His strings of broken words wound on
and on, baiting my mind
but I had followed far enough and
wanted rest from this
miss-patterned maze, I turned
my face from his disgendering malaise
and slugged my sullen bones away.

Though not convinced, I raised no cry
my conniving nonchalance just led and said:
Let him to his own little thingy
and me maybe to his young wife!

2

My nonchalance was soon nonplussed
my airs eloping with my strength
as I stepped step after step along his streets
deserted and without an eye or single soul
to be seen by any door.
Each road to me looked just the same
round those buildings angular and grey,
And the only signs were numbered strings
straining under endless digit ticks.
And concrete blocks where homes had been
and concrete blocks where fields had been
concrete blocks cemented
over virgin soil unturned.
My mind, my mind! I called my
mind but could not picture any
leaf nor conceive the
colour green.
And concrete blocks where homes had been
with the curtains torn aside, the windows were
of one-way glass I could not see inside.
And tower block by tower block, and each turn
brought more tower blocks, all fused
above my head, modules moulded
on modules, bolted atomistically
to link as a mass of
midget molecules blocking out
the clear blue sky.

My face drooped, my eye saw grey
as roads rolled old before my feet.
Grades of grey, grey chipping stones,
grit pressed into organic paste
hardened to dull darkened grist
and ground with grim in
flattened twists.

Feeling no warmth I choked to breathe
and knew that here:
Differences in temperature
had died.
The whole was only entropy.

Not warm, no wind, not cold, no dew
for devices syphoned sun and star
into black sucking holes
while from hidden subterranean
crevices was fanned
a constant vacuum cool.
His hole was hormone-entropy.

No wet, no dry, no lovers' pause,
no breath of breeze rushed through my hair
no soul set soles upon those streets
no trace of dust was ever trodden down
and between those blocks atrophied air
stayed static and lukewarm.

Then numbers coding at every bend
started deciphering for my sense:
No Stops allow
No Pause
Move On
Go further round these model roads
No Waiting
Never Play

The Child You Were
Is Long Deceased

Displays channelled my eyes to mime,
I wanted sleep and I wanted sleep
but as numbers clicked their codes
my unconscious mind commoding strobes
marched to machine-ticked time.

I wanted sleep and cursed these legs
that ever moved me on, I stared
but chanced upon no grassy verge
meeting those razor-ruled roads,
no space where moments lost their
drag in a shady sunny dale,
no gentle rise, no running deer
no fragrant woods, no rills, no rest,
no place where I at peace could lay
this beating body's burden down.

Water, crackled a husky voice
and the sound in the husk
was mine.
Drumming through that place
of fever long-extinct
the only answer pounded round
buh-bump, buh-bump, buh-bump
but rigid beat pushering my heart
was conducted by no song.

Then in a window I saw a note
words, words people had written down
some message maybe left for me,
it was not far, I ran and ran
but my limbs moved
viscous
slow,
and then I read upon that sign:
> *Here only those*
> *pricked with mRNA*
> *and stitched with pacemakers*
> *may dine*

I turned once more and wormed along,
along those old rolled roads,
amnesia engulfed my sighs
and bled my remnant self,
no memories remained to me
that other spheres also were,
that any other being was
who I would ever chance to meet.

My only comfort on those lanes so
lacking life, was this:
                        No human child
                        could live there
                        and survive.

3

Why? You might have asked
and *Why?* I said
but why I said, *Why?*
That I never could find out why
but I said, *Why?* or my voice said:
Why?
and I listened to the why I'd said.

Through those lanes where corrosion
never honed a broken heart
my voice spoke me alive.

After, *Why?* I said, *But why?*
I said, *But why?*
And stormed,
all in me imploded
to a why:
Why was I me – or why
was I?

My knees throbbed with why,
I knelt and scraped the ground,
cut and scratched my hands with why,
my breast was charred with why
my tears dripped with why,
... only what why?
What was my why?

My question wove no sound,
no words were born from reasoning
... while the meanings
of wherefore or where from
waded dark
as shadows of
abominations around
Hibernian retreats.

Penetrating that plastic overhang
some wish, beating
with embryonic life
and reflecting secret starry
rhythms unknown to my
unnamed heart,
some wish in this
nameless numb expanse,
some wish must await
my voice.

My storm had drained
through those efforts drenched
with death
to qualm-free quiet calm
when a question
centred on my lips and the words
that it wore were these ...

4

As wrappings of non-daring ego
waned to a deposit in a dream
what triflings were turned
into intensity,
what knots received the Gordian
slash of Alexander
as my grand desiring to know
broke winds
of speech, doubled up
and grunting, my guts
in cramps but on the verge …
rapacious increases in exhilaration
blazing all-expiring airs
with a fanfare of majestic elation
such as throbs through an
epileptic before a fit –
this question parted my lips:
Is Hegel still alive?

Is Hegel still alive?
With this wish to know
scarred into words
I lost myself in lethargy.
The effort to ask wrenched
me from my limbs; fatigue
floated through legs and arms
and soft cushioned neck.

This state buoyant
upon wavy surfaces of dreaming,
this state between
being and absence
loss and becoming
through which my whispers
echo:

> *Philosophers*
> *are they not lovers*
> *of Sophia?*
> *Philosophers are they not*
> *the lovers of Sophia?*

5

Entranced at the veil of slumber
my quest gradually focusing
from a life of many lives …
sequence becoming
simultaneity
budding as the very point
of insubstantiality
at the centre of a rose …

Solemnly I intone: *Philosophia*
and add, as if I were a solo congregation
coming habitually to
the required response,
For the love of Holy Wisdom.

As response to my response
a canticle floods this space
where somewhere
there is me.

Stillness in a sacred stream
all around I hear her voice
yet my senses so frail can find
no face until I
bow my head to see.

Youth's first sigh
infuses her song, fine lines
cut blood red across her cheek,
her hair, white as starlight,
is braided into three trailing
to a bow of unity,
and her eyes
are as immediate as a babe's.

Of her communication choiring
from all sides I understand
its sense but not its sentences;
her speech communes
like words I've heard
returning now to know.

A rough translation might have gone:
Prophecies she sorely awaited
with Merlin's child at play beside
waves lapping crystal-strewn
shores of the Lady's Celtic
lake to show how balance
poignantly alive between
maid and man can bear
unborn nature's blessed becoming
anew into our earthy home.

Have I chanced into initiation's
most high presence? Tracing
to my heart of hearts, her gentle smile
invites me to apprentice all myself.
How earnestly then my salvaged youth

strives to repeat her statements.
But their sense emulsifying
with after-vibes of daytime tedium
distorted the semantic,
my sounds of speech patterned
only this stuttering string of
phonemes …
Predictions its programs computed
from Kinsey-cloned reports
to classify Hegelianism as
a possible optimal case scenario
for the futurisation
of sexuality ...
My heart sobbed to hear this
sterile rasp of sounds.

My unreadiness inflicts sorrow
on her impassioned patient gaze,
that maidenly ageless
slender figure weeps
silently as a fleeting why
within her tear's rainbow chalice
questions my very depths.

A liquid pearl trickles
to her lips, she touches
that drop of pure saline pain
and stretches her fingertip to me,
it shines and she becomes
shimmering space –
refulgence petalled round
a centre rosy still

while I am swathed
in saddest thoughtful blue.
She fades or I
fade away from her.

Without mooring, tossed hither
thither, turning inwards
to bemoan this self called mine.

Through an eye I cannot see
I behold an outline
darkly by my side,
a presence I well know
but cannot name, whose face
is cowled, whose garments
are of coarsest, roughest grade.

Mournfully he shakes his hidden head
and vice-like takes my arm
and leads me sobbing
away even from memories
of her sanctuary so fragrant
and alive with the blessed swell
of living yet to be …

6

He led me far
and far away toward
the outward reel of time.

He led me on, my feet
flapping like flippers, and each
unsteady step felt as if
a month of ache went by.

I might have counted twelve
or maybe less
when walking quite by myself
I noticed how my own
tears' watery salt had
quenched my thirst for meaning and
washed away that dense
and suffocating desiccation
deposited between
the Geneticist's tower blocks.

And as I went on my way and looked about
somehow life didn't seem to be too bad at all.

Walking by myself, or so it seemed,
through a landscape's virulent unfamiliarity
where thistles thrust themselves up
with hybrid vigour among the brambles
then in a glade, a garage
which only served crude oil
and hogweed-flavoured sorbets in
upside-down turned cones
but no one was around
to till the pumps
so I went on.

My path wound further through the woods
until I came across a plaque
of monumental size
shiny black marble lettered red:
>   *Dedicated to Caesar's right thumb*
>   *On the Imperial occasion of its*
>   *Sixty Sixth Hundredth*
>   *Downturn*
Feeling in my guts that I was not alone
I ghosted my glance around
half-hidden by an oak
a lion squinted through me
a last bit of bone slightly
sticking from its snarl
or was that just the way
the King of Beasts smirks
when his belly's full
of freshly guzzled flesh?

My reaction was immediate
I thought I'd fool him and nipped
onto the marble plaque, and stood
rock-still balancing
on my right toe pretending to
be Mercury with wingéd heels.
I pushed out my jaw, opened my arms
and hoped the lion would not think
of biting the Messenger of the Gods
especially not the alabaster version
I imagined I was made of.

Trying to stay steady
but from the line of my protruding face
I could only see the King of Beasts
by twisting my eyes as far as they could turn
he had not moved –
an art-loving lion, I mused.

Swiftly becoming proud of my nifty craft
in duping man-devouring carnivores
I pouted my haughty jowls, and bethought me:
Even the King of Beasts is no match
for human cleverness such as mine.

Minutes passed
minutes passed – or
maybe time went slow
when measured by the ache
in my right toe.
I twisted my eyes again
trying not to jerk them around,

the lion had not twitched
nor had it bitten through
that last bit of bone
a tough bit, I guess, or
perhaps it's just not hungry.
Oh but of course, what a fool I am,
it must be a tooth pick
(for no one, so far as I know, has ever
accused a lion of having
dirty habits).

Suddenly a stab of pain erupted
from my right toe
and I knew my marble posture
was beginning to resemble
soggy clay; I begged
my wits to aid me
but my loins gave the impression
of being afflicted by something else
(something polite speech refers to
as diarrhoea).

Then it struck me – Modern Art!
Mercury-in-Motion!
I started to flap my arms
slowly and gracefully at first
and then with gathering speed
and hoped the lion, even
in his jungle retreat, was
well acquainted with the modernities
of dynamic portraiture.

But alas, alas, my Achilles toe
still bitched
if I flapped enough, I thought,
perhaps my arms can take the weight
or maybe with a bit of luck or the acquired knack
I could even get to fly.

My right toe, the surly swine,
wasn't quite convinced and, still worse,
it jittered with increasing violence.
Now I knew my marble end was nigh
yet what resources resound
in human nature – a last resort:
Tap dancing!

Though it occurred to me
even as I began to click
(and clicks are hard to get
when wearing wellies)
that perhaps the all-American style
might be a bit unflattering
for his ankle-winged Grecian majesty,
who at the time I still
purported to represent,
then it hit me like a flash,
how foolish, why of course,
I'd perform a Nijinsky version
of Fred Astaire.
Must keep the legs stretched ballet-like
or the lion might wonder about the puppetry –
and I knew it was vital
absolutely vital

to hold my neck and jaw stiffly protruded.
And when I looked over at the King of Beasts
I was very, very careful
to move my eyeballs round
just as slow as they would go
for I deemed his rustic Jungle-Lordship
would surely never believe
that puppeteers not even
modern ones have strings
attached to eyeballs.

Straining my eyes I noted
he had not even belched;
his tooth-pick bone still jutted
from his snarl. *It's going well*
I purred with great relief, *I think*
I've got him hypnotised.

My confidence swelled, I imagined orchestras
Tchaikovsky, Basie, Satchmo, Strauss,
I even improvised ballet to
Air on a G-string and Palestrina motets.
Ah, if only the Prima Ballerina
could see me now, her heart
would surely melt to the tapping
of my wellies. Ah, what castles
in the air, if only Ginger were here
to do a turn with me upon Great Caesar's
Black Thumb Plaque.
Then with a shock I gaped at myself
perhaps, perhaps it's just not
just not trendy enough for

his Jungle-Royalty's taste –
so I quickly switched to doing Mic's
Honky-Tonk kicks, Reggie and Rap-like
raptor twitches, Mike Jack's
Moonwalking and nearly broke my neck
with Break dancing
before going back to Classics.
Ah, how time passes when you're having fun,
already the sun was in the West and
very soon it would be time
for his Jungle-Highness to roll
his royal privilege over his pride.

Alas, my curtains came down rather abruptly
with Singing in the Rain
I thought I'd do a twiz
only the lamppost wasn't there
for my imaginary umbrella to hang on …
My nose grubbed dirt
I lay, head buried, expecting the
worst and heard four feet bounding
toward me and felt hot
breath about my neck and then
a voice which sounded like a child's:
Wow man! You were great, just great!
My uncle would give the earth to get you
performing at his all-night parties.
His grin stretched wide, luckily
with hurried reflex I shushed him
finger to my lips, *The lion*
will get us!

The two kids looked scared as I
indicated slowly, very slowly with my
eyeballs, twisting them as far as
they could go, to where the King of Beasts
stood growling with a bit of bone
stuck between his teeth.
Him! You're afraid of him!
He's a bronze, she blurted,
then frowning at me, her eyes
ancient as a centurion's
of years not of soldiers, I might add,
she poked me in the chest saying, *Mister*
if you'll do all that for stooge lion
what would you do for a woman?

Then her brother added, *Do you ever do such turns*
in gardens?

Her knowing side wink answered for me, *Only at*
night and under balconies.

I could feel my face getting beety but I jumped up
growling in a remonstrative tone sternly full of
unfathomable reticence, *Last one to put his hand in*
the lion's mouth's a dumkin.

We rushed off, me leading until turning back to
see where the kids were, I tripped over a tree root.

He's a dumkin! He's a dumkin! she shouted as if
jigging on hot coals.

Her brother was rolling on the ground clutching a
vibrating stomach and stamping with his feet.

I put my trembling hand on the lion's bit of bone
and jumped back as if bitten, *It's real, a real bit!* Two

reins went from it up to a chariot, probably Caesar's chariot. The sun was shining from behind it, I shielded my eyes and looked up at what I guessed was his Imperial Majesty: Bronze turning a greeny shade of grey but his Roman helmet was lead and his hands were hooves.

The solo figure, rearing up in the chariot and with the reins about a hoof, was a donkey. Its nostrils snorted wide above a brazen bray.

Though the bronze asinine Caesar had a leaden helm, his teeth were silver – unfortunately most of them had been removed.

Well, well, Imperial Caesar is a donkey without its two front teeth.

What's a Caesar? said the kid.

Caesar! He's a royal might, an Imperial ruler who holds the reins over many countries, whose thunderous commands rain down –

Is that why he's got hooves instead of hands, to press people down in the dirt? she asked.

His other hoof was stuck to a raised whip.

My uncle says that here the big ones plop off with flatulence almost as soon as they arrive, her brother noted philosophically.

We turned and walked slowly back to the path.

What place is this?

Oh, it's just a place, she said.

Our place, whispered her brother.

I looked carefully at him, he seemed to have grown almost up to my chest in the few minutes since I'd met him.

You kids sure shoot up quick?

It usually takes about three or four days here, she answered. *Let's run on ahead and tell them Perseus is coming.*

Yes, we'll get them to prepare a party for Mr. Parsnip.

I think I prefer the former appellation, I said rather solemnly, *But my real name's ...*

They looked up at me with urgency as though I were about to impart some profound secret.

I'm, er, I'm called, I'm called ...

I just couldn't remember my name.

Don't worry, she sympathised resting her head momentarily on my shoulder, *Most people forget their names here.*

Come on Sis, let's run on ahead.

Okay, only we can walk some of the way, can't we?

They pointed out my path through the woods then turned away and bounded off in the opposite direction.

She gave me a final glance and waved calling, *We'll see you again when you remember your name, Sir Percevel.*

Bye, bye Lord Pomegranate, shouted her brother.

They disappeared through the trees. And I went on, immeasurably sad as though my childhood were trampling the grass breathlessly beside the kids.

8
Grandmother Burning

I wandered head down away from the setting sun and heard no sound except my rasping cough and swam in the emotion of losing that innocence which once played untiringly with playful friends.

Dusk grew darker, twigs snapped under my feet. A smash of tankards rupturing a ribald song, poured over to me from my left.

People I muttered, feeling the urge to take risks as I casually approached their full-blooded feasting.

A bonfire's flames shot skyward, sparks flew impudently upwards in their lusty untroubled attempts to escape the curling smoke. Around rough wooden tables people sat drinking, guzzling, shouting and back scratching.

By the fire was a girl, a bare-bottomed damsel with knickers around an ankle; her hindquarters were being held near but not too near the fire by four young men. The crowd was engrossed in the spectacle.

Come on, singe her pubics!
Get her buttocks squirming!
Get her heat up!
Sweat her thighs out!

The poor waif was screaming – and wildly kissing her tormentors.

All this commotion, these goings-on, I confess, made me somewhat nervous, a little over-temperaturised under the collar. I scratched my neck with a fingertip. A feeling of pity mingling with my military sense of duty led me to take a step into the fray.

Friends! I called out in a loud voice feigning a pawnbroker's authority with an upraised hand, *Friends, learn to be charitable!*

A newcomer! they whooped swarming around me.

Friends, learn to offer charity.

What's his fat-assed lordship preaching on about? shouted a grandmotherly figure with a voluminous contralto and more than overgenerous proportions.

Charity! I retorted glancing sternly around, suddenly sensing myself blessed with a rising mastery over the situation as though I were an itinerant friar come to assert the law for a straying flock.

Yeah, what's that fat-assed charity? repeated the same voluminous Contralto, *Can you eat it? Not many teeth left,* she pointed to her enormous oral cavity, *But I can still suck with the best of 'em!*

We must offer charity, madam, and charity is love!

Love! I'll take that luv, love you anywhere luv, under the trees, on the table, in the tub – anywhere! You just name where you'll offer it, that charity of yours, and I'll take you up in it, see!

She pointed downwards and struggled to heave her proportions up from the table.

I sort of swallowed and put a finger under my shirt collar.

Yeah, she's still good at it, wild as a teenager, but just you watch out you don't get stuck underneath her rucking or you'll never see it out again! growled the deep voice of a navvy-like character with a reddish beard.

Somehow my sense of mastery over the situation was slipping away into the shadows.

He's mine, I saw him first! cried the girl, the one who'd, well, whose hairs had been on the singe.

She'd jumped into a tub and was now dripping all over my shoes. She put her arm round my neck and pulled my head toward her whispering seductively, *Cold water's heaven on a hot behind!*

She kissed me on the mouth then bit me where I would have had a tit if I'd had a tit.

They all began shrieking, Let the two lovers get on the job!

No, you mean, let the two charities offer charity.

My semantic grasp of the surroundings was wavering like flames of a fire.

I'm not the jealous type, grinned the grandmotherly woman waddling her proportions over toward us, *You warm him up and I'll take over – I'll soon suck all his charity out of him!*

Her grin had only a couple of dark broken teeth left. She protruded her lips at me as though they were a catfish's sucker.

All around was rollicking camaraderie. No longer feeling my preacherly instincts could stop this flock from straying, I squinted about for a comfortable means of retreating but the girl clinging to me made it a bit tricky.

Er, don't you have a husband?

We don't have house-bounds here, the men get us, we get the men, understand?

I pushed two fingers under my collar as I tried to come up with an appropriate topic for intelligent conversation.

Isn't it past your bedtime?

Weee! she yelled, *How about here?* pointing down at our feet.

I dragged my fingers round under my collar as I asked a trifle naively, *Don't you have beds?*

Beds? This is Bedland! Everywhere's a bed for us, we bed down anywhere.

At any time of night? I mused.

Yeah, or day or morning or afternoon. She snuggled up to me as she spoke, *You know it's hotter by the fire, we can get more sweat going but if you'd rather, we can find a quieter spot.*

I perked up at this and looked down into her face. Hair falling around her bare shoulders, in the firelight's glimmer, a pearl of perspiration trickled down her cheek, my eyes followed it until it disappeared down into warm curvaceous darkness between …

Penny for your thoughts, she giggled.

Penny, I repeated as if breaking from a trance.

The maid or the money? she winked.

Huh! boomed the red-bearded navvy, *It'll take more than pennies to come and buy maids in this place.*

She stamped in annoyance. *I can play a maid as well as anyone and he can come by me all night if he wants to!*

I scratched my neck with three fingers under my collar and sort of gazed about dazedly.

A number of dwarf-like characters were wobbling around, their only occupation appeared to be to grab people when they least expected it by, well, by the pubic area of their loins and cling on squealing until they were shaken off.

I had to gather my thoughts. *Penny, er Penny was the name of my first playmate. We played together all the time as kids. Then I lost her late one Summer. Her mother left town too that Fall.*

Suddenly I felt like a little kid again, I wanted to throw myself on the ground and kick and cry. The girl was smothering me in kisses. *I'll be your little Penny and keep my purse purring for you.*

I was losing myself in her wet kisses. But then I jerked my head up and said in a voice that surprised me, *Penny, Penny she was called, only not your usual Penelope, she had a funny name – what was it now ... P, Per, Per, Pers –*

Out with Percy! shouted the well-known Contralto from behind us, *I want my go too before the night's out!*

I put four fingers under my shirt collar. She was standing a few feet away, her grin transforming into a smoochy catfish sucker. I held tightly onto the girl and turned away. Little lapdogs were running in and out of the goings-on, yapping wildly until seeing me they curled up their muzzles and growled, looking as if they'd take a bite of anything which appeared.

The girl was pulling me away from the crowd.

What's your name? I asked.

We don't have names here, we don't have time, we're just together with everyone else.

But your mother, I began.

We don't have mothers. Nor children. She dropped her head sadly, *We eat a special mixture of roots and beetle bowels, and we never have children. If girls want children they leave us.*

But I can have your child if you want, her eyes were shining as they glanced up into mine.

I put my hand under my collar.

Berserker shrieks broke out. The whole mob came running up, surrounded us and sort of surged us back toward the bonfire.

A man in a long grey cloak was throwing handfuls of power into the flames, sparks of all colours flew up from it and shot around with wailing sounds before they died.

88! 88! 88! one after another shouted out.

He's drawn the Eighty Eight!

The girl looked scared.

What does it mean? I asked with a mote of trepidation.

All newcomers get a lottery number drawn for them, then they have to perform for us and, and they've drawn the Eighty Eight for you.

What's that?

The Great-Granny Suck! whooped the not

unfamiliar Contralto, *And guess who's the Great Granny this week?* She pointed to where two of her not insignificant proportions hung blancmange-like over her belly.

I put my arm under my shirt collar.

They were all jumping around screaming, *88, 88, the Great Granny Suck!*

Is there no way out? my eyes were darting about for an escape route as I spoke.

The girl grabbed me. *No you mustn't try to run away or, or everybody will have it off with you, the men as well as the women.*

I held onto her feeling as if I were about to pass out, my kneecaps ballooning. *There's no way out then?*

You could take the forfeit, said the girl.

I'll take the forfeit, I'll take the forfeit! I bellowed.

The crowd fell silent, everyone sat down. Some men rushed off and started to haul a contraption toward the fire.

What's that?

An antique milkshake machine, she whispered

A brass plate on the Contraption read: *300 jerks a minute*.

Five a second, I muttered hopelessly.

Don't worry, said the girl, *We don't have power any more, it's manual now, we can only get it going up and down 200 times a minute.*

Two men wheeled up the Contraption and set it on the right of the bonfire. On the left, four men struggled to push up a large and cumbersome rickshaw and in the rickshaw sat Granny.

Everyone was shouting:

On the machine with him!

Choose the Granny!

Attach him to the Contraption!

No, attach him to the Granny!

A man in a brown cloak was tossing power into fire from which shot up small, dark red, ember-like sparks.

From behind me a man in white standing on a table called for quiet in his bass voice. It was the bearded navvy who had changed clothes and who seemed to have become the Master of Ceremonies: *Now is the time of choosing*, he intoned solemnly opening his arms, *The Contraption – or The Great Granny Suck?*

The antique milkshake machine stood ominously on my right. Desperately I tried to work out: *How many jerks a second if there are 200 a minute*. But my mind was blank.

My eyes reluctantly transferred to Granny. Men were pulling corsets off her.

Can one try anything once? I wondered to myself.

She grinned and made her sucker at me, then she took a huge red German sausage and started to push it into her mouth. It was disappearing at about the rate of one finger-width a second.

Semi automatically I began calculating: *If sausage is gorged at a rate of one finger-width a second, how much will be devoured in a minute?*

It was all hopeless, I'd be screaming for sure well

before the count reached ten.

I shook my head in desperation, thrust both arms under my collar and gulped from somewhere inside me, *Gee, is there no middle way?*

A man in a deep violet cloak was casting handfuls of grit into the fire which transformed into white sparks flying away from the dark enfolding smoke to vanish quietly in the night air.

The Master of Ceremonies repeated, *Now is the time of choosing!*

I stood trembling but when I spoke my voice came resonant and strong, *If I choose the Granny, can I decide the place of the suck?*

With her mouth still full of sausage she chanted in her slurred rustic contralto:

> *Anywhere you offer it*
> *I'll take you up in it*
> *on the table, in the tub*
> *on the toilet, in the pub*

The whole crowd joined in with her.

It must have been Bedland's national anthem.

I stepped forward with all the sternness of a Prussian officer surrendering to the Huns, *I choose the Granny – and I will take her there!* pointing to the very centre of the bonfire.

There were gasps. Granny bit through the sausage, the remains of it fell to the ground, two lapdogs pounced on it and fought over it, ripping it to tiny shreds.

Everyone looked over at Granny. No one moved, no one spoke as she coughed up the rest of the sausage.

Suddenly lifting her arms she whooped, *I'll take him up, right up there on top of the bonfire. We've all got to go when the time comes, I'll be the suckling sow to his boaring stroke, it'll be one hell of a sizzling suck!*

Almost out of habit I reached down and took my right foot but couldn't quite get it up to my neck.

They swarmed around and dragged the girl away from me. Granny was wheeled up in her oversized rickshaw, she clasped my arm and put it to her sucker. I took a few tottering steps toward the fire, shielding my eyes from its burning heat and muttering, *I've nothing left.*

Breaking free from her captives the girl rushed to the Master of Ceremonies in the white coat and begged him on her knees to save me.

Friends, he boomed in his deep voice, *There is another way, a secret and dangerous way* – a stillness held the air in people's lungs as he paused looking long and earnestly down at the men and women, and then to me before exclaiming, *The newcomer can tell a story!*

A wave of excitement growing to hysteria stirred the flock as they shouted, *Story, story, story.* Their voices gradually merging into a single chant, *Stor-y! Stor-y! Stor-y!*

He raised his hand, everyone sat down, all were staring shyly up at me. For the first time I looked into their eyes.

Even the lapdogs sniffed toward me in a friendly

fashion.

Yes, I will tell you a story, I said quietly as they stood me on the sawn-off trunk of a huge oak. I stood looking round that circle of expectation feeling myself a hopelessly inadequate storyteller. Everything was blank. I couldn't think, I couldn't even remember my own name. Sweat dribbled down inside my shirt. I glanced at the girl.

She was gazing at me imploringly, *Give them a real two-storey story*, she begged.

No, a genuine three-storey story! said the Master of Ceremonies.

In a flood of inspired relief, a single word came to my lips, *Hegel*.

They all repeated, *Hegel! Hegel!* in rising cadences of wild anticipation.

A teenager on the front row jumped up yelling, *Isn't the Hegelian, a Kama Butt-press where the woman sits on top?*

The girl's eyes were shining upon me. The Master of Ceremonies was standing behind us. Granny dotingly pressed my left hand to her sucker.

But already my storyteller's pulse was starting to pound. Hegel, whose biography was no more to me than a vague reference in Dialecticalism, was beginning to conjure himself vividly before my imagination …

9

Naming that paragon of Idealism sent
meteor showers through my blood –
a story with spores of Freud in Jungian springs
watering almost culpable concupiscence
round Hegel's very germane hearth.

The plot: a maid
he longs for and a wife
who covers more than half the bed;
a thesis scrumptious to imagine
won within the folds … until
the antithesis flops
that weighty logic of her phenomenal
buttocks right down next to his.

By day his chair seeking the universal
bravely pronounces another logic
than relentless straight-line charges
which strictly imply Socrates
being a man is tainted mortally,
pressed from the same hereditary fruit
that patterned Adam's patent in mankind.

For Hegel in blithe endeavours
between action and reaction
dialectical presence is
potentially established, something
more than mere prediction
from the past, extrapolation

or causality predetermined comes
gently down to play, higher
qualities are given life,
higher being balanced between
innocence and experience.

His earthbound life spurned
by Grecian idyll, like ours
not Socratically alive:
to know the good and flee
from it, to know the bad and
buckle to it – his love
of wisdom is not tame,
he, like Paul, has fought
with beasts and almost wholly has
that which he would not have
and has not that which he
would have as whole.

His theses gustily disclaimed
above rows of revering student heads,
his professional presence so potent
for the hosts of adoring bachelors.
But at home imprisoned
with his papers, his pondering turns
head to tail, churns
philosophy in poetry's urn:
With trembling fingers let me undo
those clasps which hold your golden hair
let me descend into eyes so blue
kiss rosy cheeks of a face so fair

and that place with shorter darker hair –
wrathfully his philosophical nails
shred the unfinished script and tear
out strands of greying hair.

Couplets echoing with fleshy coupling
crudely intruding into lyrical allusion –
cause inner tempests to blow
because he knows the intent was
not to import images rudely nude
but to implicate and lay bare
states of psychic and spiritual
encounter.

A knock upon his study door
only she – can knock like that!
He rises knocking up
against a pile of heavy books.
He opens, she is there:
her red-golden tresses bound, neat
and tidy starched maid's uniform.
His unkempt steel-grey locks, lose-fitting
dark professional robes and dialectical
stare down between two –
If it please, sir, the Lady
of the house awaits your pleasure
at the table. Meaning
dinner is served.
His response, a rumbling
guttural cough. As he shuts
the door and shuts her out, he

wheezes, *One moment, please*.
But as he stoops over the stack
of wobbly tomes, he inside and she
lingering still outside his study,
his eyes and mouth are moist.
Over that maid whose eyes are pools
he all too often drools.

Pulses pumping in his temples,
hand unsteady on his pen
as in the library blue-grey gusts
billow from his pipe.
Nearly always out of breath
but without tobacco bouts
his blood runs round too slow.

In subtle words the thesis is laid
down while perhaps an
antipathetic swell dams up
the scorpion surge to
produce swirling eddies in
his rosy circulation down below.
His deeper pole lulled
to plodding duty-focused dullness.
Gossip-flaunters touting
their constipated wit around
conservative salons suggest
this deflammatory condition
waxes from a wane of lusty
red-blood-ruddy drive to firmly
wedge himself in
matrimonial stays.

But shaking bedroom feathers
from sweet, sweaty strains of sleep
and seeing an excessive concavity
damply dented in the boudoir set-piece
chambermaids smirk as they flirt
with fancied scenes where
without faint heart the
Hegels' nightly nest withstands
hours of pestle-treatment
iteratively looping
the espoused knot through
delicate conduits of time.

Yet who can tell, maybe
the naked truth hovers
somewhere between?

He retires late, or so the gossip says,
well, it was known his wife in younger days
drank coffee to maintain her waking ways
but now she knows her spread can take the lays
for when together in those night time stays
she can always sprawl him in their frays
while Hegel thinks it's he alone who pays.

And what desperation not to wait
within warm four-poster sheets
once the crowing chanticleer has startled
his spouse's snoring to a stall.

Because the body's dawdling dross
makes bold thoughts unliftable as lead
he longs to leave sight's cloying floss
where everything is but a thing and dead,
so as if sinking silently through moss
as if just words had justly all been said
in meaty tomes become the soul's worn boss
while invalidity vacillates in a bed
where life's to-be-or-not has all but fled
while science prints its worlds of endless dread
and life leads only back to states of being led …

He paces acute perplexity across
the study with a troubled tread
right struggles left amid a muddled gloss
as far above reactions in a smog-filled head
his waiting heeds how yearning bled.
The maiden's absence creates the misty space
where lost love's tears are freely shed
and higher synthesis awaits the hallowed place
where resolve and lucidity wed
in that unending moment of utter loss
when the dark and shining lightnings cross.

If wilder fancies shake him to a shred
and anger soils his blood muddy red
normal training returns at a toss when
he reaches for the tobacco pouch instead

A never-ending lack of interaction
by day he philosophises away
as puffing through a meerschaum pout
his pulses spin half-easy simulation –
until anon as fair eve's rose erodes
even nicotine smoulder loses its fiery taste
for lonely abidance by inner light
and then alack comes night
when from below something uncurls
to make his wishing grow.

Only scholarly longing to embrace oblivion
can keep his chary balancing upright.

The day is gone
the household chores are done
the servants doors are closed,
he slowly climbs the stairs
blowing the candle out to undress
in dark outside the master bedroom,
how his heart burns unrequited –
dare he, dare he take such sideways ways
that lead backstairs and up to where
she lies, the lithe and lovely lady's maid,
to shuffle darkly holding onto walls
while a nightcap's tassel dangles
round his skinny shoulders shiver
but each step approaches nearer her sighs
where golden tresses stray on linen white.

How will he enter – as a reckless gallant
thrusting through the maiden's threshold
or like a bear hunter grunting as he comes
from mountain ranges into the cave
or as a romantic, silent as a shrew,
twitching nostrils to take in her scent
as his fingers delicately open hers …

Miserably he remembers
how he tried such an episode once.
Three steps from the maiden's room
Fräulein Schlossmagen, the housekeeper,
caught him, out
she came at him from the shadows like
a turtle pushing from its shell a bloated neck
to curiously sniff a vagrant hermit crab.

Die Fräulein houses the keep
because her style of figure makes
the lady of the house figure herself slim
but smug figurings of relativity
are worthless, absolutely,
for one whose distress coins fantasies
of golden tresses strewn on linen white.
All Hegel knows is, it is now
philosophy must prove her worth.

Die Fräulein pushes closer,
luckily his knack of synthesis
seizes the situation's node,
he fakes naked flabbergastery,

Why, by what ways sleepwalkers walk!
and, *Oh, what an unexpected pleasure*
to meet you like this, Miss Blusterbelly!

Die Fräulein presses even nearer
and the narrow way never seemed
as tight as it seems to him just then,
angst blushes down to bluish toes
atwitch in leathern slippers.
Quickly though his dueling mind
seeks to resolve that
apparent incongruence
in synthetic enterprise,
he pretends to faint … die Fräulein
took him, bosomly,
before his body felt
the floor and gave prolonged
the kiss of life (and this long
before such first-aid knowledge was
commonly known as sound technique).
Gasping for breath
clutching a banished heart …

And well, his wife's
conversation dwelt a lot
next morn on mice,
of how there seemed to be some
infestation, of how she'd heard
mischievous scamperings upstairs
along those unlit hallways
leading through the servants quarters.

Then after dinner she proudly showed him
mousetraps procured at the ironmongers:
gruesome racks
to snap rats backs
or sever human toes.
In darkness outside the master bedroom
Hegel dares yet dares not date
the lithe and lovely lady's maid.
To dare or not to dare –
he dithers docile with cold
and partially undressed, sniffs
the air and mutters, *Cheesy.*

Thus domiciled and reconciled, and with
vague hopes of not further potentising
their four-posters intimacy,
he hobbles as a pregnant rat
across plush purrings of a she-cat's nap
toward the double-master's bed,
lies softly down and listens, listens
to a certain someone's sleepy grr
much louder than a little pussy's purr.
He lies so still yet cannot sleep
and dares not move a single toe
but every other nightly rustle sound
fans picture flames of his beloved maid's
dreamy, sighing, whying, tender sleep
where golden tresses stray on linen white.

Time passes in polarity:
his body chilled as a fugitive's

119

but inner fire afire from below,
sadly no ready appeasement
comes to hand.
Those invitations for her to study
in his study, to recline with golden
hair undone as a damsel
in distress upon his studded
leather chair and he to reach over her
and press the loose stud in …
Those invitations for her to come
into his library – did her blue
eyes answer no or do they
answer yes? And how does she
take that glint when squinting
he assesses her design?
His lumpen sense delectably reminds
how he soon may tether her in lewd confines.
Hints subtly left that if she so wished
she could be known by rite – his
logic dialectically decides
he soon may gather in those shrewd asides.

Inner sight in fever and his body
somewhere stiff, oh, the ceaseless ache
with coming excruciation on the make
for he can surely just reach out and take
as all the while the lovely lady's maid
dressed only with her tresses
is sighing in her dreams
just up the stairs …

By such byways can such thoughts prowl
that even philosophic man can learn to growl –
from academic shelving to gymnastics
in the theatres of farce his
make-belief becomes
almost believable …

Quietly, so quietly he lifts
the sheets and part of him protrudes,
a trembling heart, a trembling
limb, his naked foot touches
the woodwork with a frozen toe and
there in darkness something creaks.
The solid boards, his mental thesis states
but other things like springs
can also creak, a dalliant wife
recovering from her valiant snores
ruptures his conquistadorial zest,
fanning her cuddly conjugal
warmth she ritefully
drags him from
and to the edge.

Her rite of springs finds poor Hegel out
in such a pinch he cannot even shout
his neck nods fitfully to his doom
for now he must down under play the groom.

The creaking floor, the creaking bed
one on edge, the other on a nether edge,
so rumbled under undulating ups and downs

her crush on him squashes
his coming flight – he
a philosophic denizen at the zenith
by day, dressed down
to tumble round less proud by night.

An antithesis heaving over a thesis
until causality itself becomes
but strife. And life
compressed to a massive squirm
of titillating conflabbation
holds flatly to the four-poster's ledge.

In hours like these as Hegel's wick well knows
the tick of time just hardly ever goes.

Oh, to imagine such geistlickin' delight
with the thesis tucked
lovingly under his sight …
until antithesis lumbers
rudely over his night …
while all the while
the lovely lady's maid is
dreaming up the stairs.

His daylight brokered by nicotine
his night swamped by a shrugging nought
as time ruts her earnest song so slow
to where draped harmonies dis-pair
and dawn hardly
comes to crow.

As ever louder holster-moans
accompany his tethered groans …

Yet at the anticlimax Herr Hegel's
most eminent mind
finds itself refocused and refined,
his thinking rightly recalls
the roan: on high is light,
a maiden's golden hair waits
fair upon his waiting dream,
below in murky matters
stalk only shoddy negatives
so he concludes: Above
squelched knights and sodden
bad tobacco breath
absolute spirit must be our all.

This court of nightly sacrifice makes known
how material, so raw at the meeting's end,
sags only to emptiness.

Thus Dialecticalism, estranged
from meaty cheeks, must
deliberate as untouched spirit.
Beyond the soul's shamed pail
(and entities in apparent separation)
stands Spirit-Geist
or ghostly spiriting
whose messages in riveting rounds
of give-and-take reel

in the attainment of the whole:
The Absolute – pristine
or merely puritan?

10

Is this absolute truism or
morbid half truth?
Does not human history's dolour
demand that two polar archetypes
follow one after the other.
Spirit's dialectical transcendence
ghostly as a smoking sprite
and Materialism's blood-letting immanence
crying out from each
oppressed inhabitant of earth?

Was Hegel's bold urge to rest
the edifice of Historical Dialecticalism
on crystalline spirit's pyramid
of motionless finality
but impolarity?
Improper Yang-born blood
still seeking to subdue
breathy desires for
Yin's more mundane maul?

And must not this, reflecting
Providence's predilection
for the troubled ethos of Hegelian logic,
cobble later to itself a balance toll?

Via the stencilling of one,
dispossessed of property, of nation, land
starving perhaps but for a peaceful angel's hand,
Dialecticalism's ghostly Absolute
is turned roughly upside down,
topsy-turvied to receive
Materia's grind of economic rinds
as its only sculptured base?

Is not this counterbalance
(unbalanced in itself)
but deadly bloody foil
to ghostly bloodless haunts
of Hegelian categorisation
and the Middle European enclosure
of das Ich?

Did not Marx forgetting freedom,
his first love, also inflate
equating capital considerations
with robbery, the creaming of surplus
off the work of workers,
instead of realising new wealth provides
capacities to renew,
to bring about what has not been,
rich possibilities created to make
the future's potential present?

And have not Marxian Socialist economies
always concerned themselves with planning
from the past, while ensuring
that profits come to the people,
'People' being of course synonymous
with 'the Party' and its dacha-endowed
officer corps?
In the land where revolution flowered
in Autumn not in Spring
the Party ensured its continuing survival
by reincarnating
as the Oligarchy.
And 'the Organs' of the Soviets became
the template for the way
the Mafia goes about its business.

Marxists and scientific materialists
conceive men and women as animals
growing old, never realising each
child is uniquely individual,
a species in itself,
with potential not
predetermined by the past.
When men, women and children are
seen as countable by census
Revolutionary Terror becomes
just one more option:

One – or one million – can die
for the nation, all explicitly
erased so the rest fall

fear-filled into line
to obey unconditionally
the Pyramid of the Party,
the High Priests of the Temple,
or the "accepted" views of science.

When a non-thinking majority takes up
the accepted ideological and behavioural
norms without complaining
then those in power can plan
the future for us.

11

Wheezy bibliographic tiredness
mired under museum books and shaggy brows
agitating for short cuts to Utopian nicety.
Dreams of pantomime abstraction
with families torn apart in
the simplistic Party
Manifesto begging
for a best scenario void
for Antithesis as a ruling point
to choke commands down
the Pyramid of the Nomenklatura:
Nameless personae merely
obeying orders from the ranks above,
stony, non-revolting, faceless pestles
garbed in the non-discussable formulae
of bureaucratic necessity
crushing the mortal
Slavic man and woman.

Just for awhile of course, until
becoming needless it
dictates itself away:
Centralised ossification withers
to a pall pulling society through
a loop, a noose tightening
us all to freedom,
the freedom of corpses to decay.

A short circuit with levers
of dictatorship dangled
in the thick greasy fingers of a
people's unchosen representative.

For unopposed Antithesis
must will to dominate;
Ruthless non-dialectical centrality comes
to Stalinise
a frigid frightened world.
The mechanisms of remorselessness
twiddled like hairs of a moustache
in nicotine nurtured nails.

Daubing theoretical propaganda
under the bookworm shelves of that edifice
storing mummies for public stare,
Marx's hair grew thick and grey
about his head as gradually the holy
dialectic became intangible.
His eyes upon man-made material
surmised: Utopia's outcome
is predetermined, necessitated
by the mere movement
of measurable time.
To be or not to be –
what mattered to the man
was only the to-be
which had become.

Life infused with idea, art or
lived suffering for the unseen
was stripped of significance,
his pen pounced
on its nether part, the rest
pronounced mirage
just puffed-up superstructures,
uneconomic ideological
non-necessities.

History, germinating from abstractions
groomed in hate, splattered
red on white. Russia's childhood
dragged through jagged ruins.
Traditional life close to church bells
and the black earth scythed
by the sword while
dialectical hope asleep
under night stars circling
the endless tundra of the North
was bypassed by
that stint of 'worker' power.

Under the Party's pyramid
men and women were trained
to snoop and make report, to spy
and be constantly spied upon.
The populace bowed by bombardment
of Party propaganda.

All paths led
to the apex of the worker tower
the centre of proletarian storm
stillborn in night's eerie
insomnia, the straining
of a continent's worker power
compressed
into a single, static, sterile point:
a Marshal drugged
upon digesting
ordinary people's lives.

A Secretary General addicted
with himself
dictating through a hierarchy of scribes:
That, despite the recent Party drive
in bureaucratic scintillation,
Kulak-inspired underproduction
was claiming statistical corrections.

In the just reported deportment stakes
certain elements, the Zak-istocracy,
woke to a chill easterly reception,
some names, that is, were quietly
rubbed from live archives
and a few townships found themselves
dislodged from later maps.

The sun descended somewhere in the West
and millions statistically relapsed …
while the Lubyanka brooded
with the sighs of

bullet-induced deaths
and Muscovites masked
their forebodings of nightmare.
And we have slowly learnt
the Leninist paradise is a life
of queuing to five-year plans.
Queuing, like snails, uneasy
for toilet rolls (rationed
one rip per crap)
queuing for soggy sausage
that somehow never after all
quite found a place to rest
upon the emptied shelves
in this land of steppes where
hierarchy vacated by
angels became
a party celebrating
its Coba-webbed nomenklatura:
Heroes of the unholy union
whose dark visitations
were kept in countless
criss-crossed files.

When Spirit's tyranny over man
and Matter's tyranny over woman
part as the waters of the Red Sea,
when this silken membrane
holding Yang from Yin
awakens to higher synthesis
within the human heart,
when boundaries of worlds are brought
into focus by the human I,
when Merlin's staff crosses to defend
our germanes' spill,
when mercy returns and insight
unburdens the matter of men's time,
when the holy dialectic of to-be
or not-to-be unites
this little life of many lives,
when Hegel once more dances
meaning into the right
creative half of Marx
allowing material encapsulations
to open for the
Now in time.
When Marx's sun returns
to resolve Hegel's departed hope:
May Mahayana's caring love
shine into Nirvana's still
unpopulated night.

13

Hegel's wife's cries die
to shallow sighs
her awful weight becomes
again a woman's form, her
femininity recalls its
fledgling capacity for flight.
She whimpers wet kisses
so thankfully upon his shoulder
as though his hero-swan
had swooped upon her
like Achilles coming
to gloat afresh
over the groans of Troy.

He, a lonely philosopher
a setter-up of theses
to be flayed, and she,
his heavy stalwart spouse,
and neither an athlete …
while somewhere on high
hidden in the servants' rooms
a maid with golden tresses
dreams restlessly
on linen white.

Though in love with a maid above
Hegel looks through their cooling
curtained matrimonial cave
toward the dark shape of the

wife wallowing at his side,
a woman long since made
and quite unmaid – pity
graces his exhaustion
as he pats her hand.
Though he romances
rather reluctantly at night
something in him somehow
loves her even now.

14

My search to soothe this storm
of wordless weaving imagery
welled toward a tear –
did Hegel betray the eternal
logic of the dialectic
by committing her ultimate development
to Absolutism
by making the overriding Absolute
a spirit devoid
of nature's (and Virgin Nature's)
life-giving springs?

The Hegelian Absolute – an idol
worshipped by the intellect
or a philosophy severed
from Sophia's love?

The Absolute taken out of time
and made remote from man,
Sophia (once again) robbed
of her raiment, her holy
and most fruitful virginity denied.
Romance bled …
fatherless and motherless
who is to bear the child
to be?

Suddenly his sins were mine
together we looked from our past –
had we like so many others
bound time's birth,
neutering chronology
with that same Pharisaical knot
which once pitted
the ungrateful unbending
mortise of sabbatical rigour
(the logic of the morgue)
to crowd out and pilot love?

Our mute and penitent prayers arise
as Hegel's trauma disembodies
in that holy intermission
denoting dream-free sleep.
His face and form seem dead,
I kneel alone
to mourn the elapsing
entreaty of his latent
entelechy …
and hearken as notes of
the passing future
die
unsteadily
through now.

Hegel wades exhausted to dawn's clay
and to his own continuity in time,
my mind likewise longs to leave
these fruitless reams

dull with listless
loneliness
reflected in my dreams
but in a body torn and heavy
as a half-born thing
why do I ever burn
to know the truth he sought
which consummates the living seed
cradled
so graciously between
two antecedent joys?

15

I am a child crying in forest dell
dying for want of dream,
draped in swamp-damp air I knock
numbed fists against a lifeless, lichened
oak but no way opens save
to dread hung
as a corse
in still unfounded time.

Then from that ancient, ancient bole
sound tones of monotone,
faint tapping from inside the tree,
a lisping, ghostly slavering
as of an old man chained
with irons to a slowly
rolling stone,
wizened murmurs whose meanings
are mired in inebriate slur.

I was a wizard wandering alone
always alone and still alone
but caring for the starry circle
of our Table in night's
desolate dark dale.

Always solitary, I came
and yonder passed, I counselled
but none counselled me,
hermit-like I walked
bowed but taut as steel
teaching by steely eye.

Till once awhile beside a shimmering stream
a maid undressing seamed my glance,
she knew my faery name and wove
her arms – my senses throbbing
for ecstasy, my root
dank with secretion's urge
my I adrift in her –
her kisses coiled abreast
soft soil my recoils
to mischance,
whispering her burning warmth
to womb the very
surge within my veins
she called my blood her own
and culled me from the quest.

And I forgot
as others trod toward
their own demise,
as king and queen sodden
with warm voluptuous wine
uncowled their innocence
in drunken lust, their hidden
hearts left beating half alive
unconscious of the dirt and dust.

But asmoulder on her bounty moans
my juices stoked her every coy
and cloying sigh till whining
within her winsome, wanton ploys
my tensile sagged, my potential
seeped away, my magic
staff tossed off, the
immeasurable upright, emblem
of Druid office, sank
sans trace in that stagnating lie
... no naiad hand lifted
effortlessly from the waves
to clasp my wizard weapon's
arc of descent.

My staff shamelessly lost, sheep
dispersed in Celtic dales
while Camelot became a flooded vale
a loch where none now dwelt
and upon Tintagel's sentinel
above the bothered brine
no soul awoke in the wake
of the Midnight Sun
to hold her hope to hidden
light upon the western seas.

Slipping my foil, laying
my vitality in mould, she left
and nevermore came to my side.
When I woke, my staff distaffed
my plume pitched out for lechery
my eye adrift in dark.

141

Old age pawned for a nought,
a pedlar's porn bought
for naughty beggary
to hobble sullen as a gypsy's mule
by hamlets where dogs growled and men's
snorts sent greasy spittle to the grim
while around my chest there drew
a constricting sclerotic chain –
my erotic cheek folded
on the scaffold of an oak.
My secret life entombed in living tree
became unstinting monologue.

Our Table struck by doubt and taken
from the earth, misfortune
brought by my mischance. The Chalice
lived henceforth in each
knight's quest alone.
Men starved or craved more flesh and
wandered far from holy
Celtic shrines while women
asked where Merlin was
and whether he would come.

Vagrantly my gaze
stared out from emptiness,
I answered not but stumbled on
jaded and faded, and
fading from men's minds until –
as magical twilight lost
the misty fragrance of the morning rose
in dim and dour days to come,

Saxoning the body politic
for more Normal times –
my name as a fiery meteorite
was buried in the soil of legend.

This shade sucked from time
confined to everlasting limbo,
this shade of one who died
dying to loosen lonely stridency
astride sparse northern slopes,
yet sighing to dine entranced
cleaving to awakened dream
in southern climes where cloistered
(secret as an interior castle
upon a holy mountain)
with wine and bread and bliss
and visitations of ecstasy;
with my Visitor wedded and chaste,
in this wondrous oneness
this ocean of holy, holy sleep.

Suddenly a voice arose
human and near, the Shade's
yet not the Shade's:
My hope cannot forsake our quest
each note of music wrings
my heart, its beat a
chaos writhing to be freed
from doubt and each denial
of the sacred feminine.
I pray for forgiveness and for
forgiveness for the fairy maid who

whored and made me lose
my wizard's staff. For surreal
charms still maul my mulling
and squeeze mauve juices
from this selfsame wound where once
my loins were vulcanised to hers.

His words woke repentance
undisclosed, his
voice sobbed into clay,
the Shade's alone remained,
remained with grieving
unresolved –
while doleful shreds
ground from this whale
and baleful dread
groped round this dale.

I droned away in sleep unsnug
till as a child my tears bled
for Avalon's secret science
raped into cul-de-sac
upon concupiscent splits –
and for Dialecticalism's spirited divorce
descried from the shivering bed.

If Merlin after bewitchment in her lap
became the Dutchman flying through the sap,
surely Hegel must have known
that to which Guinevere was prone.

16

As I seek for word or image means
to disenchant with holy soliloquy
nature's cohabitation with
the human heart,
to ease the bewitchment of that
ever-turning, tightening
wheel which wrings
human ageing out
from the promises of youth,
as the cool conserve
of middle age locks
away adolescent lingering
and stubbornly fails to discern
dwindling instances
of childlike play.

As I search, the sounds and pictures ebb,
sombre ache my memories
with unhealed sore and hidden solace
and emotions compassionate
as Donna Elvira's plea yet certain
as Don Giovanni's godfather
whose handshake from the cold
of death
partakes of the living man …

I intimate how word is
becoming human
speech, how the

solemnity of sentencing
approaches
to allow my dreams
to wake –
but not before a threshold
has consciously been crossed.

17

Cramped in a sob which longs
to burst as the breath
of redness breaking
the rose's bud,
I know Hegel and Dialecticalism
are but names I've heard
never understood.

18

Thirsting for water, for
waters where my human
weight, my psyche
and my self can
freely live ...

Have I, like Arthur's wizard
near the Lady's Lake, trespassed
upon the nakedness of a Sheba maid
and despoiled philosophy
for romance?

Am I soaking in dotage
as Merlin, the magician once
besotted with a fay, who now
in the trunk of oaken bondage
ever weeps for forgiveness
and for grace.

19

I see before me the Geneticist's grinning
waxed and skin-stretched skull,
his claws cloned to rend
his seeds never pollinated, his
chemically spliced spores
dispersing far and wide to
penetrate rapaciously
innocent plant life.

And Newton with his alchemical
quests to amend that mechanic
which chained
moving celestial harmonies
to gravity's mathematically predictable
blind force –
and other abstractions bursting
from men's cerebral brains,
that neutered mechanic
tinkered by a stony relativism
which brought forth the big
and belching bang
to castrate cosmic spontaneity
and leave entropy
to be engraved in empty space ...

And Hegel cold as a ghost
beside his spouse's snores ...
and Marx swatting among the mummies ...
and Stalin making mummies of men ...

20

... when from somewhere
gentle as Bathsheba's first glance
in David's warrior eye
(or the echoes of chaste lullaby
sung by the mother of a son
fourteen generations further on)
these words breeze kindly
though my muteness:
Philosophers are they not
lovers of Sophia?

And her face, seeing in my eyes,
withdraws itself from night
and if she isn't quite
the heavenly virgin (nor
any other kind of maid)
at least she is the girl I love
who somehow has arisen
felt as the first presence
between dark and beckoning day
so real beside my sleep
before time converges
from unconsciousness
to worldly sense.

This human dwarf mining
a human form minus
a solitary rib, poised
with promise and blessed
by rills of love rippling

through unmoving limbs,
as I trembling reach
to touch
my image of her ...

the alarm clock rings
and keeps on ringing
keeps on ringing
keeps on ringing
keeps on ringing
till in a frustrated bitter lunge
of gratitude, I spring
from the weight of slightly
sweaty sheets to grey
cold and the grind
of daytime duties.

21

Stumbling to the bathroom wondering
whether I shall see her today
and if she will look at me
and wonder …

Brushing teeth, vigour
evident in the foam about
my lips and then abruptly
biting the toothbrush,
to stare stupidly
into the mirror
as I realise
how once again
I have forgotten to
say my morning prayers.

Notes

A few notes are added here to help readers not to miss fairly obvious allusions. And also to indicate a couple of my own rather convoluted 'cross-references'.

Page 74: "orcismatic" from Tolkien's orc.

Page 87: "Kinsey". The Kinsey Report was one of the first large scale investigations into sexual behaviour.

Page 103: "Pers-" with the obvious allusion to the Greek myth about Persephone.

Page 125: "peaceful angel" i.e. Friedrich Engels whose first name means 'peaceful realm' and last name, minus the 's', means 'angel'.

"robbery". Karl Marx conceived capital as being the surplus creamed off by the factory owners from the work of the employed. I see this as being obviously true for the situation which Marx witnessed in the nineteenth century where the factory owners paid their employees a pittance. The question is though whether this is true for all industrial activity.

Is it not possible for cooperatives for instance to create wealth through their industry, real wealth which makes not only themselves but the whole society richer?

Individuals can of course always hog capital for themselves (and thus in effect steal from both workers and the rest of society) but we can ask whether it is possible for capital derived from new ideas, research or other forms of innovation to be given back to society as a whole so that instead of being understood as 'stolen goods', it is envisaged as newly created wealth.

I am convinced that Marx missed what is essential in the concept of the creation of capital though I will not attempt to go into this topic in more detail here.

What does seem clear to me, is that the so-called 'planned economies' of socialist countries – are planned from what is already known, i.e. from the past, and thus the inherently unpredictable innovative potential of the future is missed.

Page 129: "edifice storing mummies for public stare" Karl Marx spent much of his time in the reading library of the British Museum. This museum exhibits mummies.

Page 130: "red on white", the bloody civil war in Russia which followed on from the Revolution in 1917 was fought between the Reds and the Whites.

Page 131: "Kulak" i.e. a relatively wealthy peasant farmer in pre-revolutionary Russia.

"Zak-istocracy". The word for political prisoners in Stalin's Gulag was 'zak' (sometimes written 'zek' in English). In my opinion the zaks were the true heroes of the Soviet Union.

"stillborn in night's eerie / insomnia" Stalin did not sleep at night.

Page 132: "Coba-webbed", Koba was the Party name of Stalin.

Page 133: "germanes' spill" with the obvious allusion to King Lear, *all germanes spill at once which make ingrateful man.*

"Marx's sun" Karl Marx was born during a solar eclipse. His 'sun', one might suggest, was 'darkened'.

Page 136: "Sophia (once again) robbed / of her raiment". There is a Christian 'legend' which tells of Sophia, the Heavenly Virgin, being robbed of her 'raiment' (of what

Rudolf Steiner and Valentin Tomberg speak of as Imagination and Inspiration) by Lucifer. The Heavenly Mater Dolorosa is thus without visible beauty and is silent without music or speech ... but she loves – and may, if we so wish it, also be loved by mankind in return.

Page 141: "the immeasurable upright" i.e. the 'upright' which unites heaven and earth. Arthur's sword is called Excalibur, which means what cannot be calibrated or measured. Excalibur is thus immeasurable. This imagery draws on the 'immeasurable' analogy between Merlin's staff and the sword of Arthur. When Arthur was about to die, he had his sword cast into the waters of the lake – and the legend tells us that a hand reached up and took the sword. Whereas here Merlin's staff sinks without trace, "no naiad hand lifted / effortlessly from the waves" to take hold his staff.

Page 143: "(secret as a holy mountain)" there is a subtle reference which very few are likely to be aware of so I will go into a few details.

Rudolf Steiner was a Christian esotericist who based his world view on the Holy Trinity and on the Incarnation of the Son of God, Jesus Christ. He saw reincarnation as being compatible with Christian truths. Indeed he saw the Risen Christ as the real Teacher of reincarnation today. Though he also sought to make clear certain differences between reincarnation as this is understood by many in the East and its Christian understanding. Steiner also saw it as his task to speak of reincarnation not only in a general context but in terms of actual reincarnations of historical individuals although he was only able to begin this task near the end of his life.

There is apparently a statement by Steiner that Wagner in an earlier life had been Merlin. Robert Powell in his

155

Hermetic Astrology books made the suggestion, based upon certain indications from Steiner, that St. Teresa of Alvia was also an earlier reincarnation of Wagner.

For those who know Wagner's opera *Parzival* the way Amfortas loses the Lance can be compared to Merlin's dotage of love for that damsel who locked the living man in the oak tree.

This is a little insight into the kind of thoughts I was tumbling around with when writing this section of the poem. Though I hope the poem can be read meaningfully without this background.

Page 148: "Sheba maid" with the allusion not only to the Queen of Sheba but to Bathsheba who David saw naked upon a rooftop and, even though she was the wife of one of his loyal servants, he had her brought to him and got to 'know' her.

Page 149: "a stony relativism" Einstein (whose name literally means a stone) and his theory of Relativity.

Page 150: "mother of a son fourteen generations on" i.e. Mary in the Matthew Gospel – see the genealogy at the beginning of this Gospel.

Tomorrow Troubling Today

Tomorrow Troubling Today

1

Who has whirled
to would have been the
while's singular
and enduring sense
which loosens
knots of time?

2

Can such a lonely self exist
lonely as a granite rock
grey upon a granite shore?
Can such a wayward self awake –
girded by a henge of shale
girdled with a wash of waves
circled by a cliff-clad coasts
white with long extinct crustacea
while ridges rise
and rise in rock
over this rigid case of self
matted with unbreathing matter
but breathing stone
and breathing stone.
Can such a tiny self look out?

Can such a dwindling I
gaze upon another shorn
of habitat, lost and lonely
like itself?

Can such a lone, lone I
say, "You"?
First-person foundling marked
for poverty,
a foundling masked
with swiftly ageing flesh.

Nature hard, restless, male,
robbed of courting dream.
A man sans muse, wizened
and withdrawn, rooted
on static stationary
stone.

Fallen and friendless
he stoops
knocking upon that locked
and bolted door
of dour daytime surface,
longing to find
the face behind her mimicry.

3

Waves crest cranial-like caves
in ancient weatherworn crags
to ebb with swirls
and nuances of grey.
Light filters
through undulating flows.
Dimmer dream-drenched
currents liaise and pulses pound
pending to hidden deeps
that ever yearn for the
source of nature's
innocent esprit.

4

His I within her eye
one poor finger bare
and cold offers
his touch to her …

5

Nature sullen, barren, froze,
yet restless in her
autumnal resting
for blue flowers still flicker
over graves
of selves
as freedom
even in the dying
sigh is sown.

6

Can this futile figure's form
dissolve its stony fast with stony meal?
Can sorrowing draw feature
from amorphous lethargy?
Can I encounter selflessly
another self?

Another self
you's I
lonely as me.

7

Freeing myself
of me, I see
struck into lifeless
red-brown and eroded soil
a tombstone
where an ego's
now forgotten name
waits to be
engraved.

8
Black Hole

Expanding vacuity,
horror vaccui
sucking, sucking
every vast or tiny
thing into
never-ceasing
non-existent
gloom.

9

Unknown to itself
a thing-in-itself
garners
with unrelenting myopia
its bare ration
of normality.

10

Man is lost in man alone
for no I can truly be
where no you is.

11

A thing-in-itself unknown
to itself
nightly laid with
pills or prescribed and patented
psychopharmacopica potions
which scalpel incisions
of imploding claustrophobia
between the pulsing blood and
rhythms of gentler breathing.

Slumber blighted by
total non-response
to that faint
and ever faithful
resonance
beckoning from beyond
sleep's subtle boundaries: The
roar and drama of that flame
afire
with night's deepest
now.

12
SSDD

Bosom uncertainties
smudge the wax
of weary day.
Successive surfaces of sense,
plastic or digitalised films
detached
from inwardness.
Each camera-conditioned
take
on my surrounds
provokes
sensation's static I-less
facelessness.

Moments reel
into neglect
as the urge to dalliance
deflates
and with a withering sense
of why
this day as everyday
wanes
into insomnia.

13

Dialogues dressing a monologue,
husks of empty phrase
shadowy in intervening phase,
dormant self-opinions poke up
to strut their merely shows
upon that musty, dusky stage
of ceaseless introspection …

While wormed with pseudo-norms
whorls of willful carcinogen
breed viral infestations
on internalised disputes.

14

This human self,
an I as bad as each,
aye as troubled as each,
who like all others
longs to cast
my own stony disposition to
sin
brutally upon those
who fall.

Can you not see, as upstanding men
stamp and vociferate
like ferrets ferocious
after tasting blood,
how with ingrown grimy nails,
their greed-blinded, socially
respected, most upright
normal selves
point blame's callous claw
at those weaker than themselves?

Can you not see
Him writing
with His finger in the sand
through two slowly grinding
swiftly swirling
millennia?

15
Realism contra Nominalism

Do individuals nominate species
or are species realised
in every separate voice?

16

Mere mating existence
or existentialism
in a man alone?

17

Womanless in loveless death
a man alone
a human stone.

A human stone trading
ploys of endless
trivia in this tedious
passing into
entropy.

19

Man is lost
in Monophysitism
for where no Second Person
is
no other being may
become.

20

From the unutterable afar
to earth's circlings with
her fellow solar spheres,
planetary panoramas shining
in space and unencompassed time
around this beautifully revolving
orb, this
sepulcher
for humanity's evolving
passage toward
extinction.

21
Momento Mori

One day that particular
tomorrow
will trouble your
today.

22

Child of the approaching hour
have I whored
raping stillborn aches
to know the good
which wandered aimlessly
in my deflated spaceless
present?

Have I today destroyed
this moment wherein two selves
can touch …
with callous turns
of tomorrow
and tomorrow and tomorrow?

23

Miming mortality
upon that membrane
between the yet
to come
and the already
gone.

24
The Prodigal

Have I through prodigal senses
sown
exhaustion?
Breezes of unnurtued time
becoming
emaciated nothingness,
emptiness
glutting swine bellies
with immediacy's
germane grain.

Unwaiting presents
which I,
the inheritor
of now,
have whirled to dry
and desiccated husk.

25

My male and female
neutered in divorce
as non-interiorised today
is annexed
by the past
and desire capitulates
to demise.

As dislike is somehow deemed
objective and repulsion pads out
the exterior of an imploding
self.

As Mars unscreening himself
swills Venus
a mush of isolation
intoxicated
with the coming-gone.

As I age
unnoticed by the time
of day
in the steady unbroken
beat of tomorrow
and tomorrow and tomorrow.

26

Was this me whose
flatulence cowered with whores
unable to face
the mystic ringing,
which traces constantly
across
the horizontal flow
of time?

27

Have I choked with vacuous
mumbo-jumbo
babes of I
bearing me anew
in these endless moments
floating past?
Have I slouched away
from being contrary and lain
flat down hearing
thoughtlessly
pitter-patters of rumoured abuse
so shady aftereffects of norm-defined
resignation
are draped with "Oh, that cannot be!"
… while repetitions thumping
out the Herod-press of
sluicent melancholy
ever seek to pulp
the mystic point
of time?

28

Where presents fall to past
as tomorrows so unnoticed
go
their yestering way,
as daytimes of this
unlamented ego
age
in a rallentando
of tomorrow
and tomorrow
and tomorrow.

29

Unfocused as falling
Autumn foliage,
acts of the anon
become
but moments past.

30

In time's earthly grave
no thing really is
for the eye which sees
all things
except the I who sees.

31

Blurred to sight
upon the slur of coming-gone,
have I ground in stone
or monologued to might have been
some promise of communal meal
which nourishes the human
spacious present?

This child who once was
and may yet be,
this cleft of I in me
(hidden by an unseen hand)
as the face of time
vanishes
to a looking back.

32

Did hunger mute
my mutinous thirsts through
mating mateless youth or
did the arrow pierce
last night alone?
That with today when I
first saw your face
I would know that love
and being loved
can truly meet.

33

Have I wiled to would have been
the while within
my human presence,
that sacred pass between
will be and was
childbearing
virgin hours
as my heart steadies
in affinity with yours.

34

Alone with my trampled
stealth and pride,
is it only this night
or each dark of day
I shiver
in blind sobriety
with my tiny and imprisoned
prayer
before the heavenly princess
yet to be.

35
All this

Lacing my abortive dalliance
all evil has touched me
and would have wound
with cloying habit
the desire in every taste and craving
to mummified oggulation.
Oozes of fixes and withdrawals
cavitising slime
in a tomb bubbling
with the lords of death.

All this had not your radiance
quivering in holy night
awakened
me in dreamless sleep.
All this had not your cross
of ever fragrant constancy
as starlight over slumber
or a lyre sounding
through the sepulcher of birth,
all this had not your touch
brought gentle turbulence
to breathe concord
in my cascading pulse
that in my own I
I may learn to see my
neighbour's I.

36

Sometimes angels
are only known
by their absence.

37
The Warrior

In duels cut by blood
and fear of being shamed,
mortal combat's raw
and thirsty clamour
on the dirt.

In dueling the warrior contemplates
the jewel of duality's
triple sense:
Approaching
from the plinth of the past
this moment presently
in motion is
pivoted
upon the peace of providence
so quietly coming
into being even
now
above the gore.

Death or victory?
Both are rewards.

38

My verbal name
crucibled
in this moment's very
passing:
The spear of destiny lances
I through me.

39
Mars

Mystic time
that point forged
in me by the burn
between the anvil
of the gone
and the hammer
of coming
swiftly
to the iron clash of
now –
that martial vigour where
I verb myself
in a chaos
of deconstructed space
and yet to be concluded
time.

40
Venus

An innocent touch
of self
descending as Bethlehem's
unseen yet ever shining Star
to engrail my quest
for you.

41
Mars and Venus

Compassion's distant nearness
recreating
in a temple of unneutered now
the I of
I-love-you.

42

Burning and unborn
between a smoldering future
and an ashen past,
my sword of action strikes
inner flame
to pacify my
presence
here
with you.

43

Promises glanced
through a farewell's pause
flame into vision:
Pictures of you reawaken
as another here-and-now
anoints
my outer daylight's
precious daydreaming.

44

Flickering in our glances
mute exchange,
felicitations
from an I who sees
the I of you-see-me.

45
Cana

Lapping water, freshly
drawn from deep, deep well
and chaliced within
this gilded silver vessel,
Sun-drenched water
not fermented from the vine
Cana's wedding wine
whispers of marital sustenance
freely bubbling
with that
without which
nothing was made
that was made.

46
The Troth of Time

Flames heavy with now
chalice my
quest to find that
holy place
from whence I came.

47

The starry present:
when touched by
I-trined night
to be truly
becomes.

48
The Chalice

Entwining stems questing
from below
toward the
Who am I?
Shrouded
with its halting
tenderly reverberating
echo:
Who are you?

Both quest and question,
the duet and the unborn third
sing that ancient
ever renascent
melody of the
Holy Grail.

49

When I
in tenderest questioning
am pregnant with
tomorrow
troubling today.

Maybe Lost

Who am I

Who am I
in the hours' habitual demise?

Who am I
in slighting phrase where
words sound loudly
over mute
and musing mood?

Who am I
in tear-filled laughter
forlorn within
comedy's subtle sense of
bereavement?

Who am I
in Winter's star-stabbed sable,
far, far infinity
camouflaged in frosty breath,
distance unattainable
dark and old.

Who am I today
tomorrow who am I?

Who am I
in memories melancholic ebb
and flow, inner pictures of a
person at once old

and very young
seeping
slowly
into forgetfulness …
or surging as a family
of dolphins in sudden flight
from the ocean's foamy surface
only to dive and disappear
into unplumbed depths beneath
unstable sense-saturated
daytime awareness.

Who am I
in time's untethered trickling
and in this sheer and gentle
quest where
question and the one
who quests arrow
into one.

Who am I – my
questioning flames
behind the sturdiness of
now
to bear even my footfall,
softly as a cherry blossom's
spiralling descent,
down onto the stony, piercing
certainty
of hallowed ground:
Who am I?

Iron Wheels

Only fingertips parted
by plate-glass kiss
farewell.
Iron wheels outpace her feet
iron wheels, iron wheels …
A hand sighs in the wind
carriages blur into landscape
tears coalesce
with Autumn rain.

A Blind Leper´s Wish

I wish or write
because I can no longer wish
nor speak as in my mouth pus
oozes from swollen sores.
Words
 are mumbles
(are they mine?)
Stumps in blotchy scar
fingers (were they mine?)
writing only with
and within muteness.

I wish a leper´s wish whose flesh
rots on his cheek
whose odour makes putrid
all other scents,
who lives among joys of men
but does not live their joy.

I wish, I wish a blind man´s wish
who yearns ever for
the face of man
but does not see her face.

I want to live, I want to love
in fair love´s inmost hour.
I wish a blind leper´s wish
where from this sightless

211

lonely cloistering
jumbled noises blare and fade
in meaningless to and fro,
where fervent murmurs frolic
far beyond a leprous reach
and voices beckon
only to retreat.

Where the living touch
is met by scab
… and nearness is
only a silent
unborn child.

A Fool's Hope

Hope cocooned in hardship,
in black space a glint
of starlight untainted
by sundry concerns and
Mordor's breeding
desolation.

Hope's absence appears
to outweigh her perennial
nativity
even as the background of spacial
nothingness
measures more
than starlit points
shimmering
in night's unblemished
beyond …
far, far above the sorrows
of Middle Earth

Sam and Frodo's numbers
non-significant decimals
in the statistical diagnoses
of the Tower of Power.

Animal Time

The sparrow dives
to the ground and darts
its glance toward a tree
then straight away toward
me, its eye and
head twitch hither, thither
here, there, everywhere
and then quite suddenly
it thrusts up and flies away.
Does, or how does, this bird
experience now?
Does it not dive toward
the present moment but
at its touch the sparrow's
consciousness is
vanquished –
only another twitch
another dive to reach
the present
and then another and another –
touching the moment only
to lose itself?
Is not the sparrow's experience:
rapid-fire chaotic points
of nervy disconnected
present moments?

What of the cow (or the bull
if unaffected by the urge
to find its female kind)?
Chewing the cud the cow
ruminates and ruminates
within the passage of the day,
she neither lives nor dies in
the present moment because
for her time goes quietly,
quietly by.

What of the lion, does she
experience the drama of
the moment?
Assuredly, for she hunts.
Before the chase all of her:
her eyes, whiskers and waiting limbs
look
to the moment of attack,
off she rages pounding into
the leap her claws
bring blood,
jaws bite –
in the moment of the kill
she lives the drama
(or the presence)
of the present.
But after gorging
how does the lion pride
himself on life?
His mane magnificent, his body

cushioned in warm comfort
he would purr the
very moment of the now
… but only falls asleep.

What animal can return
the human eye, what beast
or bird can return the glance
of human certainty?
Not the sparrow which nervously twitches
and darts only to die in the moment,
not the cow which chews
and chews and chews,
not the lion which kills, rips and swallows only
to sleep – not the ape, monkey or chimp
for their eyes are elsewhere
they cannot return my eye
(cannot mirror my I)
cannot retain
the now in time.

Animal time dissects:
lives and dies in the moment
or chews and ruminates
ongoingness
or chases and kills – only to pass
purring into slumber.
The darting discontinuity
of disconnected moments,
the continuous contented continuity,
or the hunter which longs to kill

and find its deeper meaning in
falling into sleep.

Only human time knows
unity in the trinity:
where past and future
kiss
and live together in
the spaciousness
of now.

The Game

If my karma is a game
of chess am I the king
everything hiinges on or
the swift and striking Queen
or some puny pawn worthless
except to offer in sacrifice,
no officer just one of many
others disappearing in early
exchanges. Or perhaps the
pieces are all part of me
aspects of my disoriented
disunity. Am I
making the move or staring
at the board of black
and white perplexed with
ongoing inactivity. Unlike
the game not to move is
verily to make a move.
Karma is a game with
nowhere to hide.

Karma is a game
of chess and I am
in it. The next move
is easy or sometimes
seems to be. yet its
spidery threads or iron

chains of consequence are
hard to pull away from
harder still to leave behind.

Karma can appear as a
wistful waif wandering barefoot
along some wild and wooded way
or fair maiden beckoning
to me ... I follow hardly aware
of making any choice around
that cryptic corner where she
fled and find only an
ageing whore with wide and
parted thickset thighs flush
with bushy hair between and
smelling of tossed off herring.
Behind her with cavernously
vacant killer stare a gunslung
pimp demanding payment
... how did I get here?

I look back and know (or
think I know) what happened
(or might have happened)
but where does it all lead,
where is it all leading to?
We are playing the same
game, aren't we?
What shall we call the sequential
yoke this move will generate
as its rammifications slither

on seruptitiously in
manifold frames of possibility
… pathways found sometimes
in space but mostly
only in time.

Karma is a game of chess
only the board is stationed in
ongoingness; its bits and pieces
strewn in the past and in the
future. And my own tiny bit
of now doesn't always seem
so spacious. Like the game the
moves I've made (or might have
made) are easier to discern
than the toughest move of all
the one I've now to make.

Will you play with me?
Are we sitting in cushioned
intercourse or baiting to
savagely outdo each other?
Or are we children rushing
aimlessly to and fro just for
this earthbound interlude, playing
for a little while until
called solemnly back by
that sleep of death?

Is Karma a game played
only in the night?

The night when parties, chores,
fitful fights and awkward attempts
to caress were only wavulets on
day's drowsy delirium, mumurings
waning into oblivion. Night
whose drama measures the essences
of daytime motifs in eternity.
Night where human motives are
undressed, their unspoken meanings
drawn into the dance we
all girate and spiral in.

Have we played together
you an I?
When was it now?
This time last Fall
or the Fall before
 – or when?
Didn't we meet upon a
Winter's thaw and say
goodbye as cherry blossom's
rosy white swirled in evening
breezes and I remained
watching as tiny shoots of green
unfurled and the calyx swelled
forth in delicious berry red.
Boutiously swinging on the branch
full-ripened cherries I
sadly never tasted.

Do you come here often?

Have you had toothache?
Oh, are you, are you already
leaving? So soon, I thought
perhaps we two could have –
please don't go, don't go so soon.
We might have stayed to play
but now you walk distractedly away
and cannot hear my feeble words.

It's cold, grey. Outside mists
cloy and set me shivering. Four
white walls and a painted bench
I sit here surrounded by
lifelessness. Once I had a
home. Even just an hour ago
I thought I heard my mother
whispering to me from
behind slumber's everpresent
threshold.

Fairytale

<Why?> they asked the old man
some considered wise, *<Is*
fairytale love almost
impossible to find
today?>
<It would be easier,> he
answered quietly with a steady
far-off gaze as if memories were
twinkling with times of knots untying
or of being more tightly wound,
<If we weren't so taken
with something less.>
<What do you mean?> they murmured
putting on puzzled expressions
though knowing full well
what he implied.
<Once upon a time,> he began
his glance sharply present,
endlessly far away, *<There was a*
youung man who was a
prince, which is to say here
in this muggled world he was
and ordinary person but in
spheres of sacredness he bears
an awareness of his self. Though
in truth each of us is a prince
or princess of we but awaken
to inklings from our hidden

higher self.> He fixed his eye
on each in turn as they smugly
looked around raising the level
of their chins noting how
they too were something special.
He continued, <*As the young man*
came of age many badgered him:
Aren't yer gonna do what yer dad did?
Aren't yer gonna make it like Uncle Tom?
Or get hitched well above yer
station and get a proper good
settlement – divorce can be
so lucrative, Aunt Ethel knows
a thing or two about all that!
His friends were in to putting
little things in holes and so
were all soon well and truly
pigeon-holed. He turned around
and pushed away seeming well-meant
peer-pressure. In his daydreams lived
One he knew he had to find.
He saw her not in life, only
guessed her presence threading gently
through thresholds of his imagination.
He knew not where she dwelt, if
she were poor, trapped or wilful,
born to wealth or even if she still
remained sedate in spheres far
from earthly time and its humbling
constrictions. He knew that to
attain fulfilment's gem he must

find her. Well he knew the Shire,
his domicile, and knew she was
elsewhere. And so he left not
really aware of where his eager
anxious steps would lead.>
The old man bowed his head
sitting silent for a while before
drawing breath to speak, *<In a*
far away shire she entered life
and spoke and sang in ways
so different from his own. She was
a princess meaning in the beyondness
of sleep she realised she is a
self. Thus very often felt
so different from her friends.
Their chatterings were background drones.
She dreamed of a prince yet neither
his figure or his face were clear
to her. In times long gone
princes and princesses shone
with the worth that lived within.
Today their bodies' outer form
might not be blessed with beauty.
She was though beautiful. And
feminine attractiveness is not without
its trouble. Many sought to court
her. She dreamt of doing good
of helping children to begin to
discover themselves. And of living
in ways others did not determine.>
Sadly he shook his head pausing

as if in reminiscence before going on,
<The young man lacked handsomeness
his form did not appear athletic, in short
he was the sort one passes by
without a second glance. This had
some merits for, alas, he was not
above being tempted, he too thought
of pressing a little thing in between
female sighs and shrugs. His physic
being as it was, not much in the
way of temptation came his way.
A second yearning lived within
drawing him toward the lonely
spiritual quest. Sometimes he sighed
for her he did no know, at others
he imagined leaving all to seek
the gate to spheres of sacredness.
There came a time when he
sojourned and she sojourned
and they arrived to study in
the same town. Did they
meet yet pass each other by,
who knows? A year or two
or three they dwelt there. Until
that day he noticed her
loveliness stricken by loss.
And then by chance, if chance is
a proper designation for what
draws our steps through life,
with a little group of people they
played a game together.

That night he slept wakefully
and encountered her in his dream
they kissed and as lips met the
created world was not
– aware in timeless formlessness
all was unbounded bliss-filled being.
Next when he saw her she
looked back at him and he
looked back at her. This was the
One he'd long waited for and knew
he loved. From that place she frequented
his feet would wander first
away only to spiral around and
end where the possibility was to
meet. Always accompanied by
acquaintances, surrounded by chatty
friends, never was she alone.
Entering the crowded space where
students relaxed after daily dues
and chores were done, his I
sought for her. The moment
he espied her figure's
female flow like a light
tap upon her shoulder his
glance coaxed her to turn and look
back at him. Across an ocean
of many mumblings and artificial
song they gaze – in timeless
interlude she lives in him.
Head down in a state of daze
dejectedly he stumbles away

wondering if his own insignificant
person for that precious extended
while had touched her
depths too. His judgement
slurred, she an elven-like
princess far above his own tormented slouchings.
No words he found
to speak. Months went by with this
prolonged moment: He looking at her
and she at him, ever begun
again and yet again. His grasp
of what this meant erring
in scrutinies of worthlessness,
his earthly figure measured by norms
of outer criterion. She incredibly
lovely, he a drooping nondescript.
With growing hopelessness he
decided to leave and seek wisdom's
portal in the East. A few months
respite then return. He sought to
study not to go to where she might
well be seen. One hapless evening
he came there and that which was,
was just as it had been.
A few times before he'd tried
to speak but his attempts had
floundered in spurious flurries
of burlesque. At last in drunken
thrust without delicacy or decorum
he barged clumsily in upon their converse asking
for a date. Exhibited

among her friends she answered
in negatively. His meagre feeble
hope gone, his dream finally
futile. Just once more they
exchanged a solitary sorry
glance as he passed her by
and departed. He left.
She never leaves him. Always
she remains the princess he ever
sought. Her eyes so luminous
and alive linger as a
feminine presence in his
further track through duties of
earthbound existence. Alas
the one he loves remained
forever distant dream.>
Again his head sank, long
was the old man speechless.
At length his listeners with a
sense of being cheated asked,
<Is that it, is that
fairytale love?> With noses turned
up they add in chorus, *<No*
normal person would live with that
loss, they'd move on and find another
truer love. That guy was just a
nutter twisted in his own illusionary
fantasies.> In a voice hardly
above a whisper he replied, *<That's right,*
he was not normal, his heart failed
to move on.> They squinted at him

asking *<Was that guy a real person,*
one you know perhaps?> *<One I*
know well,> he answered. *<A friend?>*
<Better than any friend I know
him.> Quietness reigned until
one of the listeners suddenly pointed
at the old man's chest saying,
<He was spinning us a yarn about
himself.> They all stared at him
then one and then another of the
listeners broke out in belly laughter.
Shaking their heads and smirking they
turned and walked away. A loud voice
added, *<We thought him wise*
but found him but a fool.>

Spiralling down from a flame
a moth tumbles
smell of burning insect

Burnt moth crawls
charred wings never to open
in mating's consummate flight

Waiting

Walking on a platform up
and down, waiting,
waiting for somebody or for
a train to take you far
from where you stand?
Resolute impatience in your stride,
no baggage to be seen,
are you not there
therefore to meet someone; a
slightly anxious quality imbues
your presence, a person precious
to you then: a grandchild,
son or daughter, a friend
from far away or perhaps an
old and half-forgotten flame.

Your grey hair less
than shoulder length
and wide brown eyes
too distant for me to ascertain
who you really are.
You remind me of a girl I
knew many, many years gone.
Would she look as you look
now – with her hazel hair shorn
of colour and cut so short?
Is your face lined with love's
and lost love's poignant, palpitating
essences, etched with memories buoyant,
blemished or suppressed?

Worried determination exuding
from your steps as you wait
upon the concrete platform for
I know not who?
Why are you waiting? For life
to bring fresh meaning to a time
wasted in your student years –
as once I wasted mine
and missed the one my youth so
eagerly, earnestly, so longingly
had awaited … and so sadly lost.
Am I waiting for her still?
I hope life knows for I
know not.

A partition scythed
into my living psyche.
I have searched so many
female eyes in cafés, concerts,
peopled city streets, looking,
ever looking for one to heal
this softly bleeding cleft
shelved deep inside my
cloven solitude.
Midst life's constantly recurring
actions a lost-child cry
echoes from my heart calling, calling
silently into the silence
of a clouded dark-night sky.
I know stars still shine
alas I see them not.

My train is waiting.
It should have trundled
from the station many minutes
earlier. Should I leave
this crowded compartment, the company
of my grown-up kids and risk
missing its departure to walk
over to the other platform where
you wait,
to find out if you
are her
or not?
If you are her – though I
know, as every grown-up knows,
such a starlit cross of paths
in all probability is impossible.

The grey-haired woman on the platform
paces back and forth. Inexorably my train
pulls out. The moment
departs. The chance,
so infinitesimal, has
passed me by.

In student years in the city where
we lived sometimes almost against
my will I would follow a girl with long
your-coloured hair, hoping
it was you. It never was.
What chance was there then
you were that waiting white-haired woman?
Yet now I wish I had reacted as an

adolescent trusting
in coincidence and left
that overfilled compartment and my
adult self behind
to look her
in the I.

Are not such star-blessed moments
as improbable as the lamb sleeping
contentedly beside the lion?

From this bypassed encounter one tot
of comfort remains: the unbelievably
beautiful twenty-two year-old you were
retains her loveliness
for me
though once hazel hair
were hoary, though wrinkles were to crease
her cheeks and stiffness hamper
grace-filled movements of her limbs.
I loved you then, I love you still.

Absurdly implausible as it may be
I wish I could know for certain
whether you were that grey-haired woman
who had in some sense
trusted providence
and allowed her feet to
arrive upon the platform at
that very hour
to wait impatiently for
me.

Lost Maybe

That moment still alive
in me, a friend pointed you out,
never had I seen such sorrow
grailed by female lovliness.
Next day by chance we
played a game of table football.
That night I wander seeking
something I know not what,
suddenly you stand before me
as our lips meet the world
vanishes – in endless aliveness
I am – and then I wake knowing
this dream is fabled treasure
never to be lost.
Next eve across a smoke-filled room
I look at you, you look at me,
barriers and worldly trappings gone,
time stalls in poignant encounter.
My head descended once more into
that stuffy decibel-blaring bar,
my norm-bound me shabbily
inferior to that luminescence
shining through your loveliness.
Shape of teeth, size of dick, for my
twenty-one year old student self
moats as deep and wide as the abyss
dividing a pauper in the Feudal System
from a princess. One or two more

pints then back to my bed in the
post-grad flat. All further studying
ends. Days by myself in the gas-fire
heated room, isolated in that
Edwardian dwelling reserved
for post-grad students. Maths papers
open before me but inclinations
to pursue their content deleted.
I am alone, not alone, your
face is ever looking back at me.
Time grinds on between hourly breaks
for tea or coffee at a student caf'
with its homely smell of fries and
jukebox vibes. Then back to that room
with your gaze lingering upon me, so near
so untouchable. An evening meal then
tramping city streets, circling, spiralling
in toward the student bar where
we may meet. I am a hobbit
traipsing through the Shire, eager
and afraid to espy star-shine
around an elven princess. My
glance wanders the noisy bar room
there among your friends, your back
to me. Yet the very second my I's
tactile arm alights upon your
flowing hair you turn and our
eyes meet – as the night
before and the night before that.
Looking at each other without
normalcy's straight-jacket constraint

this moment lives outside
outer ongoingness – you
as near to me as me –
then back to the seemingly intractable
gulf separating our everyday beings.
I did try on a few occasions to
speak to you. Once I manoeuvred
toward you as you came from
that crowded bar, pints in your hand
and blurted out, "Excuse me,"
intending to follow up by
asking you for a date.
You took the 'excuse me' to mean
'you're standing in my way' and with
a sharp offended glance dodged past me
and went your way before I uttered
another word. And then there was …
what does it matter, years
have passed, decades have dwindled by
since I finally in drunken slurry scrambled
in between your amicable conversing
and most impolitely begged you for
a date – you standing before the fool,
your friends around us smirking at this
clown – was it all done to ensure
a negative reply? I had no hope so
it had to end in hopelessness.
More than a year had elapsed since
your sadness first was pointed out to me
and our lips had met in dream.
Nothing remained except to go.

I left without even knowing your
name. Today at three score years
and ten I aver: you were
and are the One. To find you
will I have to wait until
our mortal coils unwind?

To Be Found

Memories of our initial
socially-at-a -distance
meetings freshly alive in me
as if five decades had
twinkled into yesterday.

Moments of our first, still
far from social, togetherness
stepping out of time, transiting
beyond day's elapsing hours:
Delicate dewdrops condensing
from a presence of spheres
knightly illumined by eternity.

Images of the one
you were, living flowers
daily springing forth anew
from memory's dark rich soil
and its arcane potential to
rekindle bygone encounter.

If I picture to myself
friends is not a carress
of their living essence
present in m imagery?
We are more than the
container, more than mere
biochemic matter.

Shining through my inner
vision of your erstwhile
twenty year old womanhood
not just the girl you were
but the self you are.

My life lived apart
from you, your human story
tracing through friendships
and family, through lasting
or passing fulfilments or stormy
upsets – unkown to me.

Did we decide ere birth
brought us each into earth's
heavy side of existence to
touch only with our eyes'
tactile arms and then to
disassociate following separate
karmic strands and byways
to learn to withstand the solitary
freedom of an independent self?
Or did we simply fail
through norm-fractioned foolishness
to clasp each others' outstretched
fingertips when from uncertain
heights and depths into
normalcy's dark day-night
inklings of true love's uniquely
living gleam filled our mourning
hearts with rosy innocence.

I am certain the quiet promise
etched into those timeless
interludes when our I's
met and distances dissolved
lives on as seed aslumber
in spheres untainted by earth's
ever struggling existences.

Moments blessed
by eternity
though seemingly forlorn
and far from traces of fulfilment
are never truly lost.
We will find
each other in this
or in the life to come.

Poetry Yet to Be

Are you there?
I thought I could recall
your long and ancient name:
You recited gentle lines and
I sought to imitate
and speak them with you
as I awoke in dream.

Are you human
and more than human,
Lady Poetry?
Even murmurs of your beating heart
in this muggled, struggling and muddied
human consciousness
tremble
with the purity of
falling snow.

Can I give voice
to your voice?
Can I speak
with echoes of how once
you spoke
before Babel's collapse splintered
language and erected
barriers of non-comprehending
between selves?

Breath behind whirling winds
and sobs of waifs
witness

for your word
within our stuttering.

Do you speak to me
as I seek to speak
for you,
my fair and wondrous
lovely Lady Poetry?

I have not truly felt only
imagined your maiden tresses tenderly
tracing across my brow. And I
confess to never having confronted
your living countenance, never have
I seen that sad smile upon
your angelic faery face
for veils swirl around
me to shroud
even inklings of clear sight.

Homer was blind
to the world about him
as he heard your musing
weave in hexameters.
I am hard
of hearing
deaf and mute.

Your song bearing the hush
and overtones of silence
ever eludes my listening.

Hark, I mutter
to myself but the poem still
is without words.

To you I hearken
my heart yearns to hold latent
gestures your celestial feet have left
as ethereal treasures
in rills and lakes,
in the water's tidal drift
and sylvan breezes
between forest trees where
you lightly stepped
and upon Celtic mountains where
anon you wake within
our restless sleep.

Stars are inaccessible
infinitely far from my feeble
human flame
even so is your wise royalty high
above my earthly self.
And yet as starlight touches
my night's impatient vigil
so do you shine
in melancholy's subtle
sway, you, my fair and
lovely Lady Poetry.

Time Inside Time

Is it possible to be within time,
to be inside time's inmost becoming?
For me to be within time
must mean to be within –
within what?
Not the past
for the past has gone by
so how can I
be within what has already been
and gone?
Not the future
for the future has not come
and is therefore nothing
but a not-yet-been.
What is left?
Only now.
But the now is an infinitesimal,
a divide between what's gone
and what is coming,
a boundary which makes the pico second
seem an aeon,
an aeon to the power of an aeon
to the power of an aeon to the …

A point without inwardness
is this my experience of now –
something gone, already passed even
as it appears? Or
is my present spacious?
Can I live inside a boundary?

Can I live inside the thickness
of a mathematical line?
The point of the present
can be defined by one line
crossing another. Two lines,
without thickness, cross
or spear through each other
to mark the moment
of the now.
And since time's inexorable ongoingness
is the arrow of the horizontal line
the crossing line is vertical.

As my experience of now
is spacious and as the divide
between past and future
is without space,
no thicker than the thickness
of a mathematical line,
is not my life within time,
within the now,
an experience of the vertical?

In the vertical line what is to happen later
is
already taking place
within my consciousness.
My heart is pierced
by the future,
even now I am alive
a little further into the future
and the miracle is

there is no collision.
My experience of what is to come
and what comes
is continuous coalescence,
I live the future
in the now.

As the foot treading upon the
serpent's head,
time's hidden vertical
crosses the
slithering of earthly ongoingness.

The future present
in the human experience
of now
christens nature's
crowded struggling for
existence.

In this spacious present
the monad is
conscious of life within space
and simultaneously
conscious of itself.

Astronomers who look
longingly toward the heavens
have chosen well,
for them the symbol of our human earth
is the cross over the circle,
the cross erected upon
a skull.

Chomping luscious green
a catepillar creeps toward
the chrysalis

Flames

Two candles approach
and with staccato suddenness
flame as one …
drawing apart
just as abruptly
they separate.
Each flame shines
now for and from itself
even as their fires when together
burn in beautiful union.

Arthur

Part I

1

Rigid as a jut of rock
on Tintagel's granite fast
gazing at spray from wave
breaking over wave,
bulge and surge
ebb and swell, swell and ebb,
sombre in solitude
hunched beside the ocean's ceaseless
groan … till twilight
dissolves itself in dark.

2

While my knights fend off furies
in ancient forest vast and
almost surreal
I, yoked to kingship
of this realm, fraiily lean
upon my human sediment.

3

Troubled deeper than sorrow
by this orb, this pulse
of silence present
above the cross of my
unsheathed and glistening
sword.

4

Only the elements (winds
echoing in the womb of waves
surf swirling over granite outcrop
surges gurgling in stony cleft)
only the elements (infusing
forms of faery-fire
along lonely Celtic shores)
only the elements (wavering
invisibly behind
waving boughs and leafy rustle)
only the elements
sigh
rages of sleepy gratitude
for my sceptre's secret solace
which whispers promises
to where winds wane
within cold chasm-deeps
and breath fades in
human fibre's gradual
asphyxiation to die
in the hidden marrow
as blood is ever born
anew in living hollows
of human bone.

5

Westward magenta woos
the ocean's wide receptacle
for our sky's rotund and dying
sun – red portal to a second
ethereal sea.

6

From my tower beneath the steady
homeward flight of fowls
above gardens, green shady groves
and woods settling with twilight's wonder,
within these walls man-built
of man-hewn stone
I begin my solitary watch.

Before me nature's broad way
is breached by luscious flood
but I am not of nature.
Ever before me sways
temptation
snap this sceptred unity
and die
or sleep with nature.

Slumber beckons me
toward lavish unrestrained
unconscious being.
Flow out my breath
and warmth of blood
let Arthur's skeleton
be desiccated as dust,
let Arthur's marrow
crave only cold stone.
And yet Sir Gawain and Sir Bors
each of my Table's knights
alone, weary, battle-stiff
staggering from pre-feudal forest
as tears trickle
against the gales
till each faints and falls
into fallow sleep,
forgetting and forgiving all.
How their jousts would waste
quashed beneath the passing chase
mired under muddied stumbles
glutted by low glory-hunts,
knightly victories or conquests
quick and cowardly,
wounds or defeats all seeping
away in unsung history,
each embarked quest would sink
untraceably beneath
time's thankless passing

into the mere of the
gone
as with their loss of now
adventures die.

Our knights battles would puff
nothingwards
but for this moment chaliced
in Excalibur's limitless
offering.

8

Behind my back Camelot's burghers
toss barely disguised snides
"Arthur is discouraged."
"Aye, lacking courage."
"Arthur is aged."
"Ha! An impotent king, see
even his wife prefers his courtiers'
embraces to his."
"His weapon is never battle-wet."
"It sags nodding at the soil."

Not so, my friends, and yet
I must not speak for I
hold tongues burning beneath
consciousness, I am bound.
My wife, 'tis said, lies
with my knights and not with me.

My subjects wag
with whispers of my cowardice
but I must not speak,
I must not issue forth to
broach too subtle truths
casting pearls (won
from tear-filled watches)
before burly burghers who
in Camelot's boisterous market
prattle among their snorting swine.
Nor must I slink away
retreating from those malice-soaked asides
spoken to be overheard.
I must remain in the very upright
centre of my royal calling
at that post between heaven's high
participation in sense-denuded night
and her daily disappearance
with dawn.

I must not speak, I must not
move, manoeuvre or remove
though rumours abound about my
non-emergence in the joust.
"Excalibur is not battle-scarred."
True my friends but listen,
those who may, to silent speech:
Excalibur is never wielded
because Excalibur wields.
No passive sword, cold
metal carried into combat

acted on by active hands,
no passive sword but sceptre
(unseen by self-seeking eyes
and ego-inflated selves)
my blade is the flaming upright
its forging is never finished
for in its wielding stillness
a presence knights our quests –
togetherness present
this very night outside day's
raw relief inside
the unheard passing
of each human time.

9*

*We fight and sleep – only Arthur
awake in starlit dark
rounds goodly combat to outer
reaches of the realm.
Our strivings require no proclamation,
deeds of lost knights need no squire
to brag their bravery abroad
for in Excalibur's refulgence
once burning quests and questions
of night's hungering heart
are steadfast in the passionate
presence of the now.*

10

Traversing the land
wave on wave, breeze
through breezes, wind within
the four winds, storm in
tempest, ebb in flows and
flow in time's mysterious ebb.
Tracing nature's nocturnal need
a higher hereness resonates
with the thunder of the sword
alive in stone.

11

Hung with the weight of my gilded
iron crown, my head nods
with oncoming waves of swooning –
yet even now I remember
my nearest and dearest, my Guinevere,
sighs with love for Lancelot.

Gaunt cheeks and tears' salt
alone speak of grieving
for my dream-steeped queen.
I see but call no cue
of seeing. Who sees
Arthur's sorrow bearing anon
upon the crowned bearer of the sword
drawn twice from stone?

12

By and by and ever
before me sways
this vale's sleepy lull.
Temptation partially withdrawn
and endlessly drawn out,
sweetening not to be
for nature
but not for me.

Yet to lie
dreaming
as Gawain and Bors of a
virgin's ache
in virgin womb.

13

In these lonely watches even heaven
sometimes seems to dream
or to be
a dream
a dream dreaming me
through dreams,
an image of an image reflected
in densities of death.

14

The ease to grip and rip apart
the needle's eye of unity
and slide
down
downwards
lower, lower through wells
welling lush and loose
with nature and unlaborious
scents sweaty
with conjugality.

15

Guinevere, my missing queen,
how oft have I wished to wake
and take you to me
and tell of my night's solitude
where my knight's pains become
my pain and of how their dying
quests are sacrificed
in this Immeasurable pyre.

16

My Lady white and true to night
Arthur so long has longed
for a heavenly touch of you.

17

In midnight desolation
I hardly more discern
if this is death with life
or life in death.

18
Amfortas

Was it a dream or did I hear
my own voice calling
the name of Amfortas
at the very brink of slumber?

My brother, thou sore, speared
and unpitied Fisher King,
in blind obscure night I am
awake, my blood bleeds
through the fourfold chalice
of a faint and fluctuating heart,
its flow not dammed, its rhythmic
whisper not impure,
no urges erupt to cause abscess
in too-finished flesh.

Amfortas, your agony cries out
to me from the not-yet-come
and begs me even this day's dark
to learn why, why my struggle
(as a stream of sorrow sojourning

in my pulse's never-ending beat)
does not trespass
to morass
my aching corporeal uncertainty
with wound like yours.
Wounds impossible to staunch
and ever festering.

Your bloody portrait pairs
my nightly hours with pain.
Descending beneath hearkened dark
our hurt – yours lacerate
of body, mine of soul –
sobs forth this knowledge
uncitable for sight:
My sufferings hold within my heart
only because Guinevere lies
with my nights and not with me.

Else I though king
would be unable,
else my straining station
as the very hammer of Tubul Cain
would pound in her sweet whines
and die me
to unfastness,
else would I
(devoid of Excalibur's
infallibility)
abdicate
and plunge

this seething brand
into desire's black burn
and smog would foul this
precious vale of Avalon
with countless particles
of self-propogating soot.

And gushing laughter of my queen
would herd us both
in ever stagnating circles
pawning selves in unchaste chase
where two (and neither a one)
are kneaded to a
mere oozing us,
would condemn us both to beg
for death in sleep.

Amfortas, my queen is not Kundry.

Though Galahad is unborn and the Grail
only an embryo alive
within time yet to be,
we also may dream of then
when you and I
when two, a king and queen
and each a royal, that is
a human self, can wait
(as Parsifal and Condwiramours)
through three still awakened nights:
starry, ethereal, warmth.

Two together one
yet each a unique
independent self.

Upon beatific thresholds
is hallowed
a heavenly third.
Lohengrin …

Three tears of nearness
unify
what we were
with who
our hearts will bear.

Amfortas, my queen is not Kundry.

19

Guinevere, my only romance,
I will not upbraid
if your unbraided hair rubs
perspirations of my nights.
Sleep sweetly with my thoroughbreds,
only by day give my
glancing I
such glances of your eye
to keep me unenthralled
by other women's charms,
give me dew-touches of your
morning's sweet melody
to hold back the white wine's
cunning effulgence
when, if riled by feminine smile,
my imaginary whiles
flirt concupiscently
with other women's wiles.

20

May my imaginary whiles
recall you, Lady
pristine white and sighing
for sacramental night.

21

I will wash each morn
that no tear stains my ageing face
as through this cross tormenting
day with night all remnants
of lukecool resent vaporise
within the scabbard of my sword.
Each morn I will rise
and work to love you anew
and my words, double-edged
as my blade, will never jab
myself in you.

22

Behind closed curtains come
crude jibe and jest:
"Arthur is old."
"Too old to fight in frays."
"Too old to make fay
with his fair queen!"
"He is not bold."
"Not bold enough to stand!"

They do not know of silent
sleeplessness when all eyes
close and selves breathe
with their beloved's breath,
I watch alone.

23

Our prayers incandescent
around the Measureless Sword
centre compassion and become
the High Table
of my knights' each lonely quest.

24

Here in Camelot I am crowned
my subjects heed my every command.
"Whose castle is this?"
"Arthur's," comes the answer.
No one, it seems, knows
that I, who am king, own nothing.
In nightly vigil where are rich
tapestries and treasuries of the day
gone by?

Even the silken-clad queen
sleeping at my side dreams
herself in Lancelot's strong arms
dates his potent embrace.

Nothing is mine save
wakefulness. I
have left all to stand
struck in stony poverty.

Excalibur alone I hold
and this but held in trust.
(For who may grasp the immeasurable?)
My sword is not my own
only leant for knightly
hours of remembrance.

25

Whence comes Excalibur?
"From the waters," says one.
"From the stone," says a second.
"No that luckless, rock-sheathed blade
rusted and broke in battle," says a third.
They do not know, Arthur
is not fickle
but one sword was his,
is his.
The sword I drew effortlessly forth
from spell-bound stone
glowing as celestial vision pierced
circles of Albion's well-guarded,
jewelled crown and my young self
received kingship of the realm
and guardianship of nature's
rugged shore and her valley's
faery forest ways, that sword drawn
from its tomb of stone
became brittle in few days
to break upon a battlefield.

(Only fools do not know
the sword will break
which no love sows.)

Borne to me by our Lady
of the rippling Lake this
sword (whose measurements
the starry heavens make)
is not another
but the blade-in-stone reforged,
reborn from that weapon fragmented
by the flight of time.
The same unspoken name
is etched in glowing golden runes
upon its rust-free resilience.

By day this speech is silent
its gilded lettering fades
in silvery formlessness.
Only by night along
lonely barriers of wave and rock
by water and by stone
within the sacred crystallising
of fiery breath
does Excalibur's gledeing
malleability become
the keeper of our knightly quests.

(Only a fool does not know
the sword will break
where no love glows.)

26

I can never conceive
how time sans sequence and heavy
with waves implacable,
how time in night's sleepless
hours can elapse
that grey once more lightens
into deepest, deepest blue
and birds begin to sing.

27

Between lithe swaying steps
my wife's smile hides
presentiment. Forgotten prophecies
amuse her mutely worded song.
Her singing pregnant
with presentiments
not present
for my day's continual loss
of time.

28

I know existence only
through the skull.
My body stiff moves without joy.
How may I with meaning hold
my morning or my evening queen?

Yet I almost believe a ray
from the Immeasurable has smote
my wakefulness with sleep
or how could I walk
each day among my courtiers,
my subjects who have slept with
Persephene's linger
fresh upon unfurrowed youthful
brows, my friends who look to me
as rightful king, their gaunt
and swiftly ageing Sire.

29

In Camelot's sedate gravity day's chores,
day's feasts, day's music move
relating human hours
to the sun's steady curve across her sky.
Harpers strum minor chords and chant
lays of ancient chivalry. And as our
minds accompany their song
partings of sweet romance or
calls to chilling combat
come alive
within our inner day:
Tabernacles spun for knighthood's
courtly joys are present
on imagined fighting fields

Fields which to our outer senses
are clogged with fleshless
bones beneath the turf,
bones in furloughs of forgotten rut,
bones of dismembered forefathers
today but lime for soil.

* We can envisage the poems in italics as being spoken by the
chorus of the knights of the Round Table.

Arthur

Part II

1

None of my Table's knights gather
now to tell their news.
Rarely are their names recalled
yet all know
our adventures, our victories, all
we did but prepared this time of crisis
where every Sir by self alone
this day seeks
for the Grail.
The Grail beckoning and fostering
aspirations yet to be fulfilled.

2

Even my wife, under darkened archways
of our ancient stone-cold crypt
before the altar seven candlelit,
even my still youth-fair queen kneels
begging Heaven's Queen for mysterious
intercessions of the
Sangreal.

3

None but I and the maid she
fondly grumbles about:
"And always complaining!"
"What does she say, my dear?"
"Nothing!"
"Er, nothing?"
"But the way she says nothing
makes me start complaining
about myself.
And her lineage! The
shepherd's cast-off
that's for sure!"

I'm glad the shepherd maid is here,
listening to my wife happily
bitch about her brings
me my only daytime smiles.

And last night as I strove in darkness
to hold my sword raised
just when my hands could no longer
stay steady with Guinevere tossing,
sighing and sliding her warm
thigh over mine –
I pursed my lips and muttered,
"King Arthur's queen but a fawning
receptacle for the sowing
of Lancelot's wild oats."
Suddenly that maid's eyes

vivid as stars in blackest night
were upon me … and I guess
I remembered my task.

4

None but I and the maid
Guinevere vehemently dotes on
know of my queen's silent sessions
of prayer deep in the
dimness of the crypt.
And I cannot but deem her earnest whispers
yearn for chivalry's lost dawn
and not just for a quick return
of knight escorts and the gay flirtations
that once reigned about her
for when I look and listen in these
dreary vaulted arches as she kneels
before the altar's seven candles
round the rough-hewn Celtic cross
her posture's trembling poignancy
resembles more a mother's care
than woman's languor
all allure for knightly bedding
... and of course those aftenoon rides
in the wood with Lancelot.
But wait! That maid, the one Guinevere delights
to groan about, has a way of looking
across you without quite
looking at you.

5
Arthur's Lament

Under silken cover sullenly I lie
staring at ruins near sleep's dull verge
my wife moaning winsome at my side
dreaming herself in plays of seek and hide
laughing and pouting through romance's surge
as she dons courtly dues of caress and sigh:
dallying in rose gardens with my young knights
till slides of amour drown those sunset sights.

6

Through our bedchamber, barren
as the taper's ash,
breath gestures moist clouds
of numbness over these our
half-neglected nights.

7

Our fraternity ventures, each for himself,
through wilderness and plagued infertile soil.
Though disappeared from daytime senses
a secret sacredness renews
each Sir's presence at his seat.
Wooden no longer but alive unseen
our Table's cambium retreat
breathes round breadths of Albion

inspiring each knight's courage for his quest
expiring with every cut and blow
as within the breastplate and the helm
a human self wakens
to human want.

8

Though gloom glowers
through marsh and morbid tracts, gloats
round heaving negligence,
luminous edges nightly borne
rain rainbow hues of shining life
as knights in righteous quest
hew mettled conscience
through fields of crawling things.

Though murk maims
remorselessly, mauls
unremittingly,
fragrance is freed and colours
quiver as knightly threshold heralds
the unperceived drama of
love forever
absolving death.

9

Nourished by adventure
quests, whose meaning is invisible
as light, return nocturnally
to the Shrine of Chivalry –
so secretly being
born
within Avalon's
misty welling forth of
times yet to be.

10

From flights where slight misjudgements
frieze in death,
each choice of conscience shrives
pain's bounty to a twine of light.
In combat of good 'gainst bad
through scenes of vital ever-active form
colours come to genesis,
every static stroke or defect darkens,
and every dowdy streak within the
shimmering registers a miss
of mercy where some cowardly
cringe or glory lust (or perhaps
some other kind of lust)
swayed in to hold opaque
flickers of holy inwardness.

11

Those other hazes, lounging
half aware and clinging greedily
to their renown,
dull staining lulls, distemper
in our living stream.
Our knightly current where in clear
awakened dream by deeds of
conscience rendered selflessly
are seeds sown in the holy
soil of holy night
to pyre Albion's bloodied shrouds
to purest light.

12

In undergrowths of fungal-morbid forest
the fittest struggling inhumanly
to survive as Klingsor's cripples
sever and join up, splicing
according to abstract plans spawned
by their skulls merely to
amass more coin.

For Klinsorian systems and minds
limited to strictures of the brain
nature is seen as neuter
not as she. So chemical constituents
are callously to be extracted.

Double-spirals ripped out and
ripped apart, riven from Natura's
faery-fostered alchemy.
Their goal: Manipulated grain
leprous as self-destructing lice.

Undergrowths of fungal-morbid
forest are to spread
throughout this and every other
fay-fair realm …
is this dream
or dream becoming day?

13

Dull, darkened and diminished
fettered strains
Klingsor designed.
His grasping cripples lurch
their heavy girths across
the hidden way
lifeless insensitivity
quashing the downward
flow of life.
Bio-machines retch
endless strains of undead
digit pulp.

14

Who hears through the ringing echoes
of sword on shield
as human hearts pound
above the gore?
Who listens to battle furies?
Who heeds lonely tournament
where youth's first eager flush
with manhood's starker self
gives way to warts and wounds
and byways beckon passing lives
... pastimes in nameless
undergrowth, mazes
sullen with similarity
whose only decider is the I?
Who gathers unfinished quests
of our forgotten nights
as we endure to furthermost straits –
homeless knights suffering to staunch
torn peripheries of Albion?

15

Contests wrought to protect
plundered vestiges of Albion await
Excalibur's stern chastisement.
Its razor fire cleaves
good from bad, leaves
boundary where verity
is gleaned and viciousness
vanquished, frees selves
from motives enslaved
by libidinous sloth and dreary
slushes of inconsequence.

Its fire raises
knighthood's nightly path –
every fearful, feckless, feeble lunge
or leer impaled on pseudo-stature,
unconscious chaff around
long-conscienced grain,
cindered
well before ways weave
that starry spiral womb
which announces
to Camelot
her child to be.

16

Not old, cold metal in emboldened
hands, not Arthur
but his poverty in prayer
cradles
the immeasurable centre
of the Table Round.

Seeds of day-quests resound
within sleep's unseen
spaces as the needle's I rings
unpredictable phases of transition
and night's heavenly periphery
is reborn
within the point.

17

Deep within our frays only
pity cups life unborn,
only mercy can tender presence,
can pass tenderly to be
present: Raised
in sacrificial upright
nature is undone (the serpent held
within the spine)
the snake of time caught
above the rend of battle
by each human bearer
of the Mosaic Staff.

18

Each knight harbours a portion
of the presence, a portion of
the promise – No! no portion
but the whole for unreservedly
the Sword Immeasurable radiates
within each true knight's star.

19

Hidden in hollow depths of human form
Excalibur mettles human marrow:
the Midnight Sun ensouled
in unfilled space
as knightly threshold gledes
the dark with light.

20

Battle wounds caught
in the brine of empathy arise
with alchemical patent ...
rainbows retrace
recondite ways toward
Chivalry's unsited origin.

21

While hearts pine
homecoming penance
morbidity flees
the proximity of the light
which sees.

22

Rainbows sigh
for Heaven's silent arch.
Acts, whose numbers
can never account,
obedient when chaliced
by Arthur chaste beside his queen –
a higher reign repeals
imbalances in mediocrity,
horizontal additions and subtractions
quantities clinically celebrate
disappear in the crucible
when a flower's tiny
pollinated seed becomes
a shoot of the
mustard tree.

23

From the realm's far reaches
impoverished of all that's won or lost
our quests return
to Chivalry's recondite beginning.
Dark opened by unselfish sight,
colours shimmer
around the sacrament whose altar
is invisible light.

24

As sword steel clashes
heights ring in depths,
Excalibur, echoing the
immeasurable moment
of the Midnight Hour,
carries our future into now.

25

Hours of patient compassion bless
knight-combat's lightning response.
As time is moved
by non-reciprocated eternity
the coming blow is known
before it strikes.

26

Who is worthy, who
not fearful
to stand or fall prostrate
beneath the firmament, that dome
fermenting knightly quest
through white incendiary heat
to tensile steel?
None has the worth, none
the weight to await
that weightless pyre
but shackled with cares and burdens of
the daytime realm Arthur is
crowned and must
rein in returning wounds
... when thresholds are lost
to night and our hours'
quotidian lukecool crawl
slowly begins.

27

Arthur steadfast in the day
of conscious night – lesions
of office liaise
to the core of time –
he trembles
before that boundary which bears
the utterness
of now.

28

Our only staff of nighthood
the Sword Immeasurable testifies
to the miracle of man,
of man who walks in nature
drinks her waters, tastes her fruits
but he is not of nature
for in Excalibur's flame
nature is undone:
Human substance becomes
the miracle of earth
and unknown night alights
within today.

29

Excalibur
our only staff of knighthood
drenched with a linger of
the human form divine.

30

Where is our Sword's crowned guardian?
Arthur watches
dead to night in day he knows
the miracle of man –
of bravery, of wounds, of lances
of all we through our combat-quests endure
to defend our dying world
as one by one we trudge
lonely toward
my-time-to-die.

31

Beside him lies his sleeping queen
does she help? Whose wisdom
is wise enough to know?
But Arthur knows
his office doomed, our quests
to perish all unless,
unless another steadies the ague
of his ageing grip.

32

Arthur holds
the Miracle of Man.
With tears so helpless
in an old man's I
his poverty perceives
this single hope:
the Miracle of Woman.

Guinevere

1

Last night I saw
or is it every night I see
my king's isolated vigil
as against lack of firmness he
strives to hold upright his
unsheathed sword.

Ageing in taciturn loneliness
he knows me
not.
He thinks I am too fatigued
with courtly ways of courting on his knights
to court with him,
too preoccupied with fantasies of
Lancelot to feel his need
of piercing concern, his tiring
manhood's rage.

How deaf he is
to my laughter peeling
through our chamber as I lie
with him, above him, undoing
the wilful stiffness of his day.

2

As his resolve begins to ebb
as his resilience loses
tensile mettle,
as he glances at my sleeping form
and a pearly tear glistens
in his I
then my laughter smiles
I too am peace-filled beside him.
As his hands hilted
with impatience tremble
mine I place with his
and take his sword's beaten warmth
into myself – quiet, quiet
beyond our motion's tenderest tremor
I am with him more awake
than he (though in his dotage
he believes I snore).

3

I entwine to open
with inwardness the
martial line of fire,
with Guinevere's help
Excalibur lances to a chalice
begging heavenwards.

4

How long have we sought together
Arthur and Guinevere –
long, long before we knew
our search rested
on but one hope …

How foolish his complaint that I flaunt
my queenly offices around
with his young officers and use up
my days only (as he falsely construes)
to languish in sleep's soft sighs
while he so mustily
insomnias his nights.

Dotage, my Lord!
Your sight sees day's senile sense
mine night's ever
youthful star.

5

And his petty jealousies of Lancelot,
does he not realise Guinevere
is childless and children
come from somewhere?
My affections for my Lancelot
bear my love for our children
those babes we never yet
have held.

6

Rachel weeps
for her children
because she so long
like Guinevere
was childless.

7

By day I imagine my Lancelot (and how often
have you not, my ageing husband,
called him your son!)
I picture him far, far from our home
riding into battle for adventure.
By dreaming dark I see him anew
his son, with wings upon his shoulders,
hovers near. This son promises
his appearance to me
in faith then I follow
falling into deepest slumber
releasing the Guinevere
in Guinevere
to night's maidenly vigil,
lonely too for from Arthur's side
comes not a sigh of thanks.

Though from elsewhere I sense
sacred echoes lightening
our task as Arthur's angel runes
with Guinevere this arch
planted with awe in the
star-filled firmament.

8

All night we labour
and just ere morn recalls
her Guinevere
I kiss Arthur's tears
drying on his sweat and
thank him for his help.

Too quickly, it seems, my daytime
puts my night to sleep,
my soul drifts lightly
with the billowing cloud
and hums with songs of birds.

While from our bed Arthur drags
that stiffness in his legs
(and that sop between them)
to his dim sense of day,
hiding in courtly silence
bitter reproaches against his wife.

9

As day further undresses
my night, I engage in courtly
manners, performing all courtly
service for the Order of our knights
with courtships (seen and unseen)
spelling rounds of courtly amour.
My flirtations rousing
one to red-blooded emotional
flagellation, while leaving
suicidally sad
another of our knights.

10

Sometimes stricken
by the shallowness of courtly conceits
my longing to conceive surfaces
and I stray upon lonely ways
toward the lapping waters and otherworldly
linger of our Welsh lakeside.

Was this the Lake from which
the Lady brought forth Excalibur
– or was that tale but
fairytale made up by Merlin before
dotage took him, dotage for
that fay-fair, sunshine-singing maid
(who could have been, and who knows
maybe was, his great-great granddaughter).
She left him worn out, senile
sans sense and voiceless
trapped within the mighty oak.
A most fitting cell, I deem,
for lecherous old men.

11

Winds and mist-clad hills surround
this lonely Celtic mere.
I have commanded my maid to wait
upon my waiting from afar. Yet
why do I wait beside this water?
And who is that maid
I took into my service? And when was it –
recently or long ago?

My memories toss me hither, thither,
whither I know not where … I am
unable to recall if they
like lake-waves come fresh as the moment
or endure ancient as the sea
swirling over granite rock.

She was colourless, quiet,
lowly birth for sure
and somehow I can never be certain
why with my word, I
affirmed her stay.

As afternoon draws on and Autumn
crests of colour weave
into the light over this lake, and
yet another night with Arthur looms
drawing down its drawbridge
like a key about to lock a
chastity belt,
as we once more strive to hold
upright to the star-signed heavens
this sacred vessel (still
believed by him
to be an iron sword).

Such labour and he so tacit
and thankless! Oh, painful
painless bed with a husband
without a tongue
who opens his mouth only to
gawk and not to kiss
our nocturnal nearness
with dialogues
of tender nestling.

13

My tears salty as the sea
slip into the ripples washing
my cold and icy, naked feet –
why Arthur do you leave
Guinevere to herself
as I, childless, surround myself
with sporting attentions of young
gallants. Wait! Is that
the shepherd maid coming to her
Lady Guinevere with some sore news
some message from I know not where
to wake fresh woes. But
can she still be so youthfully
maiden after all these years or
when was it now
she came to serve?

14

Is she smiling? I feel her
smile as the lightness of a lay
never yet blessed by human voice
or a song recalled from youth's
limitless effervescence,
or that melody upon my lips this morn
which teased fresh saline flows
of childhood's joys or sorrows
and left me in wonder
so later I pondered if just as
Arthur is blind to the sight of
sleep's awesome otherworld
perhaps I too fail to hearken to
angelic presence above this
sword transformed into a
chalice by the night.
Am I, Guinevere, deaf to harmonies
metamorphosing our vessel to a
sceptre for the realm in
midnight's hour?

15

She approaches, her movement
grace-filled as gestures of
moist warm breath,
unhindered as a silvery
fish darting against the current,
certain as rain falling
to the earth. Her footfall
feathery yet firm and so decisive
that I have seen her shoeless print
indented into rock
as if she'd pressed it
upon damp soil.

And her fleetness – Arthur has sworn
she drifted through the hall leaving
her glance upon him, even though I know
she was bending behind the hedge cupping
dew-filled roses in her hands.

16

My mood quickens when she's near
thinking becomes vibrant and alive
poised, meek yet open
to unsuspected nuances
of transposition.
Sometimes I think I only think
when she is by my side.

But where is she? I must dry
my glistening lids before
she glimpses her weeping queen.
I will not play the drooping
adolescent under her gaze.

17

How long have we unknowingly
and half-knowingly sought,
apart by day beside by night,
for our one aspiration – that this
chalice forged of hope
in shame and falling
heavenwards
be blessed by a single ray
of that which knightly song reveres
as the Sangreal …
Yet only emptiness, it seems,
fills out our everyday.

18

I wander through the Great Hall
sombre in these sorrow-drenched days
and deprived of flowery decoration,
the harper's harmonies no longer heard.
Each time entering I seek
to avoid the awkward sight of
Chivalry's rotund relic
today without a knight at any seat
yet never yet have passed without my
heart violing wild exultation
as unbidden my eye rests
upon that chair where all our
hopes are placed.

Even while passing
swiftly by
I am prostrate
before the Siege Perilous.

My husband too, how often
chancing unawares
have I met him in the Great Hall
sunken on his stool, his I
enthralled
his eyes mutely and so sadly
pondering
the Dangerous Chair –
and we embarrassed quickly
gone our separate ways.

Oh why, Arthur, is your love
for Guinevere just so much
hoarfrost? (Sometimes I think
it were better for us all
if he put his own ass
upon the Perilous Seat.)

But no, I am called
to be queen. I will draw
with my ageing king beyond
night's bridge to newest day
– though emptiness seizes
every mourning for our sons
(and for my Lancelot).

20

I will aspire to remember each child
pursuing the holy quest.
It will be according to heaven
I shall fill my nightly raiment
and dare to take my place beside
Albion's sober solitary king:

At that space in time where
Arthur weds his Guinevere
our marriage cup offers
to the firmament
the free untainted future
of maid conjoined with man
that every knightly wound and sore
may heal.

The Lady's Maid

1

I am the Maid disguised
as lady's maid
to serve Arthur's queen for his knights'
sickly realm.

2

It is I who release
Guinevere from dynastic gossip
and that courtly dalliance
dominating the melodramas of her day.

3

Oh, queen for Arthur's nights
I am the saline tear in your smile
the dew within your shining eye
and resolve's undetected
touch
trembling in your sighs.

4

I am Celtica
bereaved of the voice of bards,
widowed, mute and waiting
beside mountain, moor,
and forlorn solitary mere.

5

The Druid spirit sacrificed
to wean the present
from the past
so the lightning strike
can thunder from what is
yet to be.

6

I lead your straying steps
toward lonely lakeside dreams
with rippling waters
rivulets cold and clear
misty faded colours
of Welsh hill and dale
reawakening love
for Arthur's so neglected nights.

7

I no longer inspire poetry or music
even my sobs for that suffering child,
my cries for man
resounding in the angelic empyrean
bring no pause to heady plans
of servile politicians
and their banker-lords.

8

My voice is silence,
for each knight of the realm
(and each brawny burly burgher)
must be free to heed
or not to heed
night's missing memory.

9

How many in their sleep
weep at my hem
only to wake and turn forthwith
from wonder to the world
of monotone and calculating motives?

10

How many
in this tear-sodden vale
know
each and every human soul
is exiled
from her heavenly home?

11

How many know
the night is in travail
to bring to birth
the day to be?

12

I am midwife
for the mood of questioning.
Maid or man
how will you encounter
answers
if you have no question?

13

I am midwife for
shining clouds invisible
to sense-seeing eyes.

14

I am midwife
for the forgotten faery sight
lingering near wilder ways
at the dawn and dusk of days.

15

I am midwife for
for lost Celtic light
and the ethic of ethereal retreats
unnoticed
by the sense-clenched I.

16

I am midwife for
the magic altruism of adolescence,
for the freshness of the child
slumbering in maid and man.

17

How can you live so parched
so stunted and shorn off
from the one
who you once were?
How can you exist
deprived
of idealism's bubbling springs?

18

My tears fall upon the five
evergreen paths to wisdom's
ancient recondite pool.
My tears trickle
for human egos,
for adults barred from childhood's
holy sleep.

19

I am midwife
for recognising Easter
radiance.
Effulgence invisible
to the sense-drenched I.

Easter radiance
as unclaspable
as love.

20

Beside the loneliness of Celtic lochs
beside minstrels brooding with Celtic myth
I whisper with song.
My voice, unheard, in chorus
with the beating heart
breathing overtones
from bardic nights
as nature's living pulse
permeates
daytime senses
and pain is pregnant
with the birth of selves.

21

I am the breeze between
these lapses into ordinariness,
the Mere's surface moved
by wind to waves
my sighs of troubled yearning
wed
ethereal temperaments
to the drifting
away of worldly hours.

22

Beside the hymnal solitude
of waters and of wind
I am Vivian
Lady of the Lake
bequeathing
spontaneity in selfless love.

23

I am the Lady of the Lake
in my hands the Sword Immeasurable
is unsheathed,
in silence
deep as night in day
Excalibur arises
from the waters of life.

24

The sharp and glistening mettle
departing Arthur's aged
battle-torn and dying limbs
is thrown high above the waves …
the two-edged blade is borne
into the water's bosom,
clasped by my hand
the Sword so measureless
is sheathed.

25

I am the Maid
disguised as maid
to serve Arthur's queen for
his nights' sake.

26

It is I who release
the Guinevere in Guinevere
from courtly dalliance
and her dry mundane days.

27

Oh, queen for Arthur's knights
I am the sunrise
smiling through your tears
and true love's secret touch
upon the threshold of the quest.

28

I am your guide to truest union,
marriage – the mystery
immutable between
fair maid and man her mate.

Two, in trust to time,
love
in eternity
as night's hallowed heights
open for the sob of
human hearts.

29

I am Rachel
weeping for my children,
shedding saline dew
for every earthly man.

I am Rachel
maid to the Virgin
of Israel
and sweet mourner
for the Now in time.

30

I am Isis who
since the return of
Easter radiance
within the
gentle passing away of time,
may lift
this very eve
the veil which hides
the ever-burning flame
of Now.

31

For I am the Lady's Maid
handmaid of Mary Sophia
the Mother whose Son
has suffered
and is suffering still
the cross
of Gethsemane's eternal bloody night.

I am maid to
Mater Dolorosa
Handmaiden of God.

Appendix

Who

Is history deceased
or is its presence torn?
Or who
this day is being born
from the rosy boon
of ethereal night?

One Will Die for the Nation

Was it a tense mistake or did I,
dreaming through that gap of dark
connecting consecutive days,
hear echoes of that same sneer
hissing conspired prophecies
under the cover of most
respectable and affluent
backyards …

The Answer

The answer
to the energy crisis:
the fire which burns
without consuming.

Threesome

If Moses spoke of Him
He is the
I am.
If each unique
I
comes into being in the
Father's bosom
then the human
I am
becoming conscious of itself
in the awesome, inexorable
flow of milleseonds into millenia
must live within the
spaciousness of
now.
Not Hinduism's eternal now
where independence is maya and mirage
but the now alive in time.

The roomly, expansive location
respiring
in this moment's present
passing
away
is founded on the I-am deed,
the Cross shining though
lacerations, mockery, thirst,
loneliness and utmost pain
upon the Hill of the Skull.
Through this Event the now's
dying sorrow unfolds
within and beyond machinations

of ongoingness.
An arrow spiritually aware
crosses and conjoins
not only with the universal
(history's onward stream)
but with and within each
unique human life.

Freedom lives
only in the now.
(We cannot change
yesterday's choice
or take the hidden way
tomorrow.)

The I am spoke to Moses
from the bush burning without
ash. The I am
died – or was born –
upon Golgotha that I am
becomes the birthright of every
human I born to shed
joyous saline tears
copiously on earthly
stone and soil.

But what of ourself's further
mission? To bring about a
home not only for itself
but for each and every
struggling dirt-mired hankering
of incarnated man.
Man: men, women and children
living on earth and in

realms invisible.

Home
is a cleansing of
karma.

We forgive tiny trespasses
and are forgiven our own murky
blemishes where conscience was
sold out and trodden visiously
underfoot. To loose conscience
is to let slip away my own
precious humane identity.
To live without conscience is
to live without a self.

We can be here
only because our family,
humanity, indulges
on earth
standing upon, enjoyinng nature's
wise and wonderously beautiful
infinitesimally and infinitely
fruitful expaniveness.

Where is our home really?
Is it not alive even now
in what is to come?

The future cradles a
new heaven and new earth ...
unrealisable without us seeking
spiritual sight over and beyond
mindful awareness of mundane

everyday existence.
Not only I, not only I am
but I am here
for you, my beloved,
my beloved human neighbour
my beloved angelic neighbour
my beloved nature beings.

The future bearing an
earth yet to be
… unrealisable
without participation of the
Holy Third.

May we not only recall
our celestial origin,
may we not only be aware
of our self selflessly joining
with spiritual qualities weaving
around us this
very moment,
may we not only live
for future vision penetrating
surfaces to spheres still
coming gently into being,
but kneel recollecting the
Three
in their Sophianic unity:
Ex Deo nascimur
In Christo morimur
Per Spiritum Sanctum reviviscimus.

May a Star shine on our parting